Tadeusz Różewicz

new poems

Translated from the Polish by Bill Johnston

archipelago books

Archipelago Books
232 Third St., #A111
Brooklyn, New York 11215
www.archipelagobooks.org

Library of Congress Cataloging-in-Publication Data
Różewicz, Tadeusz.
[Poems. English. Selections]
New Poems / Tadeusz Różewicz ; translated by Bill Johnston. – 1st ed.
p. cm.
Contents: the professor's knife – gray zone – exit – recent poems.
ISBN-13: 978-0-9778576-3-0
ISBN-10: 0-9778576-8
1. Różewicz, Tadeusz – Translations into English.
I. Johnston, Bill. II. Różewicz, Tadeusz. nozyk profesora. English.
III. Różewicz, Tadeusz. szara strefa. English.
IV. Różewicz, Tadeusz. wyjscie. English. V. Title.
PG7158.R63A2 2007
891.8'517 – dc22   2007060658

the professor's knife was originally published in Polish by
Wydawnictwo Dolnośląskie as nożyk profesora in 2001.
gray zone was originally published in Polish by
Wydawnictwo Dolnośląskie as szara strefa in 2002
exit was originally published in Polish by
Wydawnictwo Dolnośląskie as wyjście in 2004.

Distributed by Consortium Book Sales and Distribution
http://www.cbsd.com

Cover art: L'homme qui marche by Alberto Giacometti

This publication was made possible by the Lannan Foundation
and the New York State Council on the Arts, a state agency.

This publication has been subsidized by Instytut Ksiazki –
the © POLAND Translation Program

Printed in Canada

Table of Contents

exit

recent poems

the professor's knife

the professor's knife

I

a freight train
cattle cars
a long string

passing through fields and woods
green meadows
grasses and wildflowers
so quietly the buzzing of bees can be heard
passing through mists
golden buttercups
marsh marigolds harebells
forget-me-nots
Vergissmeinnicht

this train
will never depart
from my memory

the pen rusts

flies off turning lovely in the light
of awoken spring

Robigus the almost unknown
demon of corrosion – a second-rank god –
consumes tracks rails
locomotives

the pen rusts
flies off sways rises
above the earth like a lark
a rusty
smudge against the blue
crumbles
earthwards

flics off
to warm lands

Robigus
who in antiquity
ate metals
– though he never touched gold –
consumes keys
and locks
swords plowshares knives
guillotine blades axes

rails that run
parallel
never meeting

a young woman
flag in hand
gives a signal
then disappears
into oblivion

toward the end of the war
a gold train left Hungary
left for the unknown
"gold"? the name was given
by American officers
mixed up in the Affair
they knew nothing
had heard nothing
besides they're dying off

gold trains amber rooms
sunken continents
Noah's ark
maybe my Hungarian friends
know something about the train
maybe its *Kursbuch* survived
its last schedule
from besieged Budapest

I stand in the last car
of the Inter Regnum – a train
to Berlin
and I hear a child nearby
exclaiming

"Look, the tree's running away! . . .
into the woods . . ."
the engine carries the children away
I open my book
a poem by Norwid
I am building
a bridge
to link the past
with the future

The past is today,
but a little further on . . .
Beyond the wheels a village is there
Not just somewhere
Where people have never gone!

freight trains
cattle cars
the color of liver and blood
long strings
crammed with banal Evil
banal fear
despair
banal children women
girls
in the springtime of life

you hear that cry
for a single sip
a single sip of water

all of humanity calls
for a single sip
of banal water

I am building
a bridge to link the past
with the future

the rails run
parallel
the trains fly past
like black birds

they end their flight
in a fiery oven
from which no
song rises
into the empty sky
the train ends
its journey
turns into
a monument

across fields meadows woods
across mountains valleys
it races ever more quietly
the stone train
stands
over the abyss

if it is ever brought to life by cries
of hatred
from racists nationalists
fundamentalists
it will crash like an avalanche
onto humanity
not onto "humanity"!

onto people

II
Columbus' Egg

years later Mieczysław and I
are sitting at breakfast
the 20th century is ending

I cut bread on a board
spread butter
add a pinch of salt

"Tadzio, you eat too much bread . . ."

I smile I like bread
"you know" I reply
"a slice of fresh bread
a slice a crust
with butter

or lard with crackling
and a little pepper"

Mietek raises his eyes to heaven

I bite the crust
I know! salt is unhealthy
and bread is unhealthy
(white bread!)
and sugar! that's death . . .

remember "sugar fortifies"?!
I think that was Wańkowicz's
Wańkowicz . . . Wańkowicz
we were a "world power"
sugar no longer fortifies . . .

do you fancy a soft-boiled egg
asks Mieczysław
if you're having one I will
an egg for breakfast sets you up

Mieczysław is standing at the stove

Tadzio! don't talk to me
while I'm boiling the eggs

why not . . .

just because! . . . now I've gone and forgotten
how many minutes they've been boiling

don't you have a watch or clock or something
a timepiece I mean we're entering
the 21st century there are supermarkets internets
there are egg timers
or whatever they're called
in modern households
in Germany
they have all kinds of gadgets clocks
that chime send signals give warnings!
they have these special devices
in which you can boil a whole egg
without the shell
in the kitchen they have microwaves or maybe it's
short waves it's all a mystery
to me one day Mietek we'll be eating
virtual eggs with no yolk
because yolks are unhealthy
not us but our grandchildren

Tadzio! you have to understand that boiling
an egg requires attention
concentration even
it'll probably be overdone

the Germans now the Germans are mechanized
mechanical eggs

mechanical or metal
music not something for us

so then?!
what?
what do you mean what
how's your egg
let's see
you taught me
how to open an egg
I used to tap the shell with a spoon
but you cut the top off
with a single decisive
slice of the knife
of course with the egg in the shell
you won't make a mess with spoons and fingernails

how's yours?

mine's good
not too hard not too soft

what was it you did . . . before you put the egg
in the water
I saw you pricking it
with something sharp . . . a needle?
I'd never seen that method
before . . .
I knew it! mine's hard-boiled

I think you're using too much salt

well you know a soft-boiled egg
without pepper or salt . . .
there are certain principles . . . and as for
the matter of timing my aunt had
a way of measuring it a soft-boiled egg is done
in the time it takes to say three hail marys

but that's not a good method for atheists

says the atheist?

what atheist . . . have you ever met a real atheist
or a real nihilist in Poland

there've been plenty
freethinkers atheists
materialists communists activists
marxists even trotskyists
what do you say to that?!

I say they were all jumping with impatience
to join the pilgrimage
of the cultured and the artistic
from Warsaw to Częstochowa
that was always the way here
everyone had their own Jew or their priest
everyone contained a Father Robak
a Jankiel or a Konrad Wallrenrod

where did Konrad Wallenrod come from?

I don't want to worry you but you've over-salted it . . .

you know there are blanks in the memory I know
listen I cannot for the life of me
remember how it was with Columbus' egg
Columbus stood the egg upright? how did it go
was it that he stood the egg on the table "on end"
we should check in Kopaliński

you have your method and I have mine

scrambled egg with sausage or bacon
is out of the question now

I remember now what Norwid said
at the Matejko exhibition in Paris
in 1876 (I think it was) you know for the last two
years I've been immersed in Norwid I intend
to write a little book
learning Norwid or learning from Norwid
Norwid said about one of Matejko's paintings
– I'd missed this though I know
almost all there is to know about Matejko –
Norwid called it "the scrambled egg of the nation"
it was *Zygmunt's Bell*
I don't know where the painting is now
from the Palais de l'Industrie (in 1873)
Scrambled egg of the nation! between

ourselves neither Europe nor America knows
what real scrambled egg is like
that's the truth . . . but how's it going with Norwid
it's not going . . . or rather it's going ploddingly
Art is like a flag on the tower of human labor

he's extraordinary . . .

III
SHADES

in the afternoon we visited
Hania's grave
Hania passed away five years ago
Mieczysław was left on his own

Robigus the rust demon
covers the past with rust
covers words and eyes
the smiles
of the dead
the pen

we walk further to the tomb
of Bronia Przybosiowa
her funeral was attended
by daughters and grandchildren
from Paris New York

Julian wanted the elder daughter
to be a gardener an orchard-keeper
he probably dreamed that in his old
age he'd have his own little apple tree
and would write
avant-garde poems
in the shade of the apple

in the shade of the tree

that he would continue
his profession – the profession of Czarnolas
but
metropolis mass machine
brought the avant-garde
an unpleasant surprise
turned into a trap

the transports set off

freight cars and cattle cars
laden with banalized evil
set off from the east
west
south and north

freight trains
crammed with banal fear
banal despair

to this day the faces
of old women
are streaked with banal tears

after the war miraculous images wept
and so did living
women

figures wept people wept

IV
THE DISCOVERY OF THE KNIFE

Mieczysław in a letter to me
from 1998
after I'd asked him
where the knife came from

whether he'd made it himself
found it
stolen it
dug it up
(the iron age)
whether it fell from the sky
(miracles do happen)

Mieczysław:
I thought some more
about that knife of mine

made from the hoop of a barrel.
It was kept in the hem
of your striped prison uniform,
because they confiscated things
and it could cost you dearly . . .
And so its function
was not only practical
but much more complex
(we should talk about it some more) . . .

Robigus coats the short iron knife
with rust
and slowly consumes it

I saw it for the first time
on the Professor's desk
in the middle of the 20th century

strange knife – I thought

neither a paper knife
nor a potato peeler
nor a knife for fish or meat

it lay between Matejko and Rodakowski
between Kantor Jaremianka and Stern
between sheets of paper
between Alina Szapocznikow
Brzozowski ("Tadzio," "Tazio")
and Nowosielski between

lectures and index cards
"strange knife" I thought
I took it in hand
laid it down again

Mieczysław went into the kitchen
to make tea (he makes strong
dark tea that I have to
dilute with hot water)

another twenty years went by

"strange knife" I thought
it lay between a book on cubism
and the end of criticism
he probably uses it to open envelopes
and in prison
he peeled potatoes
or shaved with it

that's right – said the Professor –
potato peelings could save you
from dying of hunger

order ruled on the scholar's desk
just as in his mind

you know Mieczysław I'm going to write a poem
about this knife
years passed

our children went to school
grew up graduated

it was 1968 . . . 1969
a human set foot on the moon
the exact date I don't remember
in Poland there was the memorable "March"
the March of "let writers stick to writing!"
someone caused me to stop writing . . .
I was sleeping at Mieczysław's
he lived in the building
of the academy of fine arts
on Krakowskie Przedmieście
a foul evening police zomo
patrol wagons white batons
long white batons in the fog
helmets shields

the next day I met
Przyboś at Zachęta
what is it these students want he asked
he seemed surprised taken aback
then he began to explain to me
Strzemiński's theory of the afterimage
"students"
he said as if to himself

I went back home Mieczysław's daughter
Asia asked me over dinner
"what's to be done? . . ." but I had the sense

she knew better than her father than Master Przyboś
and than me . . . what was to be done . . .
I answered "we need to stay calm"
Asia smiled . . . left

Mietek was in the hospital on Szaserów Street
he'd come round from the anesthesia
I was alone in his studio
on the walls familiar paintings
Strumiłło Nowosielski Brzozowski
a self-portrait by Mietek from the occupation

the knife lay on some newspapers

at the airport I read the slogans
writers stick to writing zionists go home
(or was it the other way round?) after I came
back to my native region
those slogans . . . smacked . . .
(smacked? of what?)
Aleksander Małachowski
asked me to do a TV interview
I spoke about how that step
the human footprint on the moon
would change the world and its people . . . I was naive.

V
THE TRAINS KEEP LEAVING

from memory now

to Oświęcim Auschwitz
Terezín Gross-Rosen Dachau
to Majdanek Treblinka
Sobibor
into history
The sidings
trains leave
from small stops
from central stations
turned into Art museums
Hamburg Paris Berlin
here artists
create their installations
trains
locomotives rusting on
closed railroad lines
Robigus spreads rust
on rails signal boxes switches
soccer fans and draftees
vandalize cars
celebrating the happiest day
of their lives
the end of their service
others are taking the oath

they kiss the flag
parents wives fiancées in tears
the band strikes up a march

but the train
that I see
(with the eyes of my soul)
has rebelled
and left the railroad tracks
the rails the lights
the switches

it's crossing green meadows
country lanes grasses
mosses
water
sky
clouds
a rainbow

is this Treblinka already
I'm asked by a young
Girl
in the flower of youth
I recognize
her lips
and her eyes like a posy of violets
it's Róża from Radomsko . . .
"I named her Róża
since a name was needed

and so she is named"
what she was really called
I don't remember

The train crosses
pads
of silver and green
moss
through woodland cuttings and clearings
forests
of the righteous and the unrighteous

surely it's Alina I think to myself

Alina the sculptress
student of Xawery Dunikowski
in a cattle car
opens a window
leans out kisses the wind
closes the little window that is disfigured
with barb wire
I'm sitting so close
that our shoulders are touching
"I've got something in my eye"
I lean forward
I have a clean handkerchief I say
pull back your eyelid please
we conduct a small operation
without anesthesia
she smiles at me through her tears

please don't be afraid
I say
it's only a speck of dust

I've performed such operations
many times
you're my guinea pig miss
(she doesn't know that she'll remain
a guinea pig)

all done I say
the tears will wash it clean
I wipe her eyes
here's the culprit
I show her a sharp black
speck of coal

allow me to introduce myself
my name is Tadeusz
I'm Róża . . . Mama and I
are on our way from Terezín to Treblinka
Mama's in the dining car
they separated us
her car is at the other end of the train

we're getting out at Treblinka
you know sir I'm dying of hunger
I'm really dying
I'm so hungry
I could eat a horse

or a carrot
a turnip
a cabbage stump
. . . and where are you going sir? if I may ask

me? nowhere special! to the woods
to collect mushrooms blueberries
get some fresh air

I'm a Satyr
the girl laughs

I can tell you the secret now
I'm getting out at the next stop
my unit is stationed at a place called
"high trees"

VI
The Last Age

I looked at the knife
it could have been for cutting bread
a knife from the iron age
– I thought – from a death camp

The iron age was last
truth shame and honor vanished
in their place were
fraud deceit trickery violence

and pernicious desires
the land once common to all
as the light of the sun is and the air
was marked out to its furthest boundaries
by cunning man . . .
Now harmful iron appeared
and gold more harmful than iron . . .

the knife
made from a piece of hoop
from a beer barrel or some other barrel
has a handle
ingeniously
curved

Hania the Professor's wife has passed away

when the Professor sits with eyes closed
when he is silent thinking writing
preparing a lecture
moving away from criticism
toward mathematics and philosophy
or perhaps logic and mysticism
he recalls what he did
with the knife in the camp
cutting bread dividing it up
saving every crumb
he did not peel potatoes
(but did not throw away peelings

as they could save someone
from starvation)

years passed
we count up
together we are
a hundred and sixty years old

the 20th century is over . . .

the Professor lives alone works does not sleep
listens to music
I came to Ustroń
from Radomsko
from memory from the past

I came to Ustroń
in July 2000 from Wrocław
and Kraków via Wadowice
I wanted to see the hometown of the poet Jawień
I was moved to see his hills his clouds
his family home the school the modest church

Dawn Day and Night with a Red Rose

you gave me a rose
red
almost black inside
autumnal

it stands out sharply
in the empty white
room
as if carved
with a lancet
by Doctor
Gottfried Benn

at night the rose
describes its shape and weight
in fragrance

it rouses me
with its thorns

cast
from sleep to a waking
that is still tremulous fluid

I see it

basking in the sun
unfolding
predatory

in its vicinity
it tolerates
neither nightingales
nor poetry

Hafis umdichtend hat Goethe gedichtet
"unmöglich scheint immer die Rose
unbegreiflich die Nachtigall"

with my eyes I touched
the compact
places
between the petals

the next day
at dawn
I took the rose
into the other room

at last I could get down
to my poem

in the presence of the rose
it had been fading away
before my eyes

secure now it took on
color
perked up

I'd realized that poetry
is jealous of the rose
the rose jealous of poetry

after a few hours
with the muse
I opened the door

I saw a black rose
gazing at itself in the mirror

it had lost none of its dignity
or significance

I took from the rose
its reflection in the mirror
and turned it into words

and in this way
I completed
the deed

[2001]

gateway

Lasciate ogni speranza
Voi ch'entrate

all hope abandon
ye who enter here

the inscription at the entrance to hell
in Dante's *Divine Comedy*

take heart!

beyond that gateway
there is no hell

hell has been dismantled
by theologists
and psychoanalysts

has been turned into an allegory
for reasons humanitarian
and educational

take heart!
beyond the gateway
there is more of the same

two drunken gravediggers
sit by a hole
they're drinking non-alcoholic beer
snacking on sausage
winking at us
playing soccer
with Adam's skull
beneath the cross

the hole waits
for tomorrow's deceased
the stiff is on its way

take heart!

here we will wait for the final
judgment

the pit fills with water
cigarette butts float there

take heart!

beyond the gateway
there will be no history
no goodness no poetry

and what will there be
stranger?

there will be stones

stone
upon stone
upon stone a stone
and on that stone
another
stone

[2000]

Ghost Ship

the days are shorter
the sundial stands
hourless in the rain

the sanatorium emerges
from clouds
like a vast passenger liner

columns of black trees
drip with water and moonlight

the sanatorium sails away
in the November mists

it rocks
its windows darkening one after another
plunges into shadow
into sleep

while below
underground
the devil has lit the old stove
in "Little Hell"

don't be afraid
it's only a late-night spot
a café

the saved and the condemned
cheeks flushed
lap up what's left of life

the temperature rises
and everything whirls
in a dance of death
um die dunklen Stellen der Frau

the ghost ship
runs aground

the mystery of the poem

once somewhere
long ago
I read a poem
by Eminowicz
whose first name
I subsequently forgot

this was before the war

then

for half a century
I never encountered
his poetry

he would come to mind
every few years
then return to oblivion

Chess?

yes I read the poem
in "Pion" magazine

chess? not *chess*
chess
I think it was *chess* the poem

rattled about in my head
like a death-watch beetle
(that was all I needed!)

two years ago
I found myself in Kraków
with Czesław Miłosz
in Ludwik Solski's Dressing Room

Mrs. Renata (this was her idea)
was asking us questions
about poetry youth the occupation
and women (laughter)
the topic was our love poetry

all at once I digressed and asked
do you remember the poet Eminowicz

Miłosz did

"Eminowicz? his first name was Ludwik"

later we talked about Staff and Fik
Czechowicz Przyboś Ważyk

a year passed
I was looking through *Extracts from Useful Books*
and on page 207 I found a poem
by Ludwik Eminowicz "At Noon"
strange poet

strange poem neither good nor bad
the vanishing poet
lived 1880–1946
I rush headlong . . . the roiling water golden
the sky suspended from a burning frame . . .

I rush headlong

Mr. Ludwik Mr. Eminowicz
wait up
don't hurry so
don't run away
from us
into a fragile immortality
in some reference book
or anthology

in October 2000
I was at the Frankfurt Book Fair
(Frankfurt am Main)
eight hundred publishers
or maybe eight thousand publishers
were exhibiting a hundred thousand new titles
a million books
"the pope of German literature and criticism"
put in an appearance
five hundred poets (of both sexes)
read their poems
ja ja lesen macht schön
(schreiben macht häßlich)

but the greatest success
was Boris Yeltsin with his bestseller
and with champagne vodka and caviar

I was there too with a small volume

I drank a glass of red wine
with Leszek Kołakowski

I read poems with Miłosz
Nike sprinting before us

suddenly Eminowicz
popped into my head
"I rush headlong . . . the roiling water golden
the sky suspended from a burning frame"
I smiled to myself
Nike running behind us
cheeks unhealthily flushed
and I was thinking about Eminowicz's poem
in "Pion" (*Chess?*)

somewhere once
long long ago
I had read that poem

[2000–2001]

rain in Kraków

rain in Kraków
rain
falling on the Wawel dragon
on the bones of giants
on Kościuszko Mound
on the Mickiewicz monument
on Podkowiński's *Frenzy*
on Mr. Dulski
on the trumpeter from St. Mary's tower

rain
rain in Kraków
dripping on the white Skałka church
on the green commons
on the Marshal's coffin
beneath silver bells
on the gray foot soldiers

the clouds hunker down
settle in over Kraków
rain
rain falling
on Wyspiański's eyes
on the unseeing stained glass

the mild eye of blue
a thunderbolt from a clear sky

long-legged maidens in high heels
fold colorful umbrellas
it's growing brighter
the sun
emerges
I walk from one monastery to another
seeking the dance of death

in my hotel room
I attempt to hold on
to a poem that's drifting away

on a sheet of paper
I have pinned a purple copper
butterfly
a patch of blue

rain rain rain
in Kraków
I read Norwid
it's sweet to sleep
sweeter to be of stone

goodnight dear friends
goodnight
living and dead poets
goodnight poetry

[July 2000]

gray zone

cobweb

four drab women
Want Hardship Worry Guilt
wait somewhere far away

a person is born
grows
starts a family
builds a home

the four specters
wait
hidden in the foundations

they build for the person
a second home
a labyrinth
in a blind alley

the person lives loves
prays and works
fills the home with hope
tears laughter
and care

the four drab women
play hide-and-seek with him
they lurk in chests
wardrobes bookcases

they feed on gloves dust
kerosene mud
they eat books
fade drab and quiet
by icy moonlight
they sit on paper flowers
the children clap
trying to kill moths
but the moths turn into silence
the silence into music

the four drab women wait

the person invites
other people
to christenings funerals
weddings and wakes
silver and gold anniversaries
the four drab women
enter the home uninvited
through the keyhole

first to appear is Guilt
behind her looms Worry
slowly there grows Want
baring her teeth comes Hardship

the home becomes a cobweb

in it are heard voices groans
gnashing of teeth
buzzing

the awakened gods
drive off
importunate humans
and yawn

. . .

on the road
of my life
which has been straight
though sometimes
it disappeared
round the bend
of history

there were whirlings

on the road of life

where I walked
flew
limped
losing along the way
the truth
which I sought
in dark places

sometimes on that road
I met
the children of my friends
my own children

I saw them learn to walk
I heard them learn to speak

in their eyes were questions

mysterious children
from the paintings
of Wojtkiewicz
hiding in corners
listening to our conversations
about poetry art music
at times they squealed
smiled were silent

mysterious children
from the paintings of Makowski
flat little clowns
with stuck-on
red noses
with snotty noses
smiling

we gradually lost our self-assurance
("what are you gawking at?")

we were so busy
then all at once
we saw that our children
have children
that they have
failures and successes
that they are turning gray
they ask us

"what are you gawking at?"
but we are silent
and hide in corners

[2002]

gray zone

"What makes gray a neutral color? Is it something physiological,
or logical?"
"Grayness is situated between two extremes (black and white)."

WITTGENSTEIN

my gray zone
is starting to include poetry

here white is not absolute white
black is not absolute black
the edges of these non-colors
adjoin

Wittgenstein's question is answered by Kępiński

The world of depression is a monochromatic world
dominated by grayness or total darkness

in the darkness of depression many things look
differently than in normal light

black and white flowers
grew only in Norwid's poetry
Mickiewicz and Słowacki
were colorists

the world we live in
reels with color

but I don't live in that world
I was only impolitely awakened
can one wake someone politely

I see
a ginger cat
in green grass
hunting a gray mouse

the artist Get
tells me he cannot see colors

he distinguishes them by the labels
on the tubes and tins

he reads and knows that this is
yellow red blue

but his palette is gray

he sees a gray cat
in gray grass
hunting a gray mouse

he has impaired vision
(he doesn't suffer from depression)
maybe he's pretending
so as to provoke his students
and enliven our discussion

we go on talking about *Bemerkugen über die Farben*
W. talks of a red circle
a red square a green circle

I say to G. it would seem
that the square is merely filled
with red or green
the square is square
not red or green
according to Lichtenberg few
people have ever seen pure white

drawing may be the purest
form of art
drawing is filled
with pure emptiness

thus a drawing
is by its nature
closer to the absolute
than a Renoir painting

the Germans say
weiße rose and rote rose
for one who doesn't know German
a rose
is neither rote nor weiße
it's just a rose

but someone else has never heard the word
rose and what he holds in his hand
is a flower or a pipe

Regression in die Ursuppe

in the beginning was a thick
soup which under the influence
of light (and heat)

produced life

from the soup emerged a creature
or rather something
that transformed itself into yeast
into a chimpanzee
eventually god came along
and created humans
man and woman
sun cat and tick

humans invented the wheel
wrote *Faust*

and began printing
paper money
all sorts of things appeared
doughnuts Fat Thursday
platonic love pedophilia
national poetry day (sic!)
national rheumatism day (sic!)
national illness day – it's today!
finally I too entered the world

in 1921 and suddenly . . .
atishoo! I'm old I forget my glasses
I forget that history
happened Caesar Hitler Mata Hari
Stalin capitalism communism
Einstein Picasso Al Capone
Al Qaida and Al Kaseltzer

during my eighty years
I've noticed that "everything"
turns into a strange soup
– but a soup of death not life
I'm drowning in this soup of death
I cry out in English
help me help me
(no one understands Polish any more)

I clutch at straws
(someone else has seized the day)

once long ago
the St. Francis of Polish poetry
Józef Wittlin
wrote an anthem on a spoonful of soup
but I forget what kind of soup it was
all at once my wife
comes out of the kitchen

she's more and more beautiful
"will you have supper with me?"
"I've already eaten" she replies

if I were Solomon
I'd create for you
the song of songs
but even Solomon can't pour
from an empty vessel let alone
a poet from Radomsko!
(not Florence or Paris
but
Radomsko . . .) Radomka
my homely little river
little creek or creeklet
creaklet? After turning
eighty I'm no longer bound
by the rules of spelling
. . . Tadeusz my friend
why exert yourself so?

I've lived to see
chat rooms columns
at-signs portals
I stare at the big dipper
above me
and don't know what to make of it
I stare at the little dipper
and think dipper or shipper

Goethe's grandson was magnificent
what was it he said?
. . . ich stehe vorm Kapitol
und weiss nicht was ich soll!

while his grandaddy had to write
dichtung und wahrheit
and add the entire *italian journey*

bravo! bravo! for the grandson
it's time to return to the primordial soup
brother poets (and sister
poetesses too!)
let's return to the anal phase
therein lies the source of all
fine arts and coarse arts
tertium non datur?
oh but yes! datur datur
the tertium is arising
before our very eyes

I know nothing about you

I don't know who you have loved
I don't know what kind of child you were

you're a young woman
with a beautiful face
alluring eyes
and a mouth that denies it

I don't know what you dreamt in the night
where you were this morning

running late
your cheeks rosy
breathless
you sat at the table

a third person came along

a young man
in a garish sweater

you were enjoying your żurek soup
or maybe it was barszcz
I had finished dinner
and was having a tea
with my finger I drew hearts
on the white napkin

Madame Maria
turned 92 today
she told me yesterday that
once in a train she met
Sofia Andreevna Tolstoy
she saw Tsar Nikolai and Rasputin
she's still not sure
if the October Revolution
made any sense
after all the Russian intelligentsia was
the most progressive in Europe
– "between you and me, Mr. Tadeusz" –
yet it was consumed
by the Revolution
" – don't forget
the newspaper and the toffees –
I wrote an article about *White Marriage*
'Who's Afraid of Tadeusz Różewicz'"

snow was falling
I thought you'd say goodbye to me
but you were on the steps
talking with the guy

I had a rough night
a bad black day
my son heard voices
he was abducted
god came to him in the form of light

a good quiet lad
he found himself in the middle
of the burning bush

bleeding
I walked through a wall of snow
heard a voice:
mein Vater, mein Vater,
                            und hörest du nicht
was Erlenkönig mir leise verspricht?
Sei ruhig, bleibe ruhig, mein Kind!
In dürren Blättern säuselt der Wind . . .

in this city
where a polar bear roams
where I hear Kiepura singing
la donna é mobile
where polar bears live
drink vodka and say "fuck it!"
and when they raise their heads
we see the faces
of our compatriots
purple as methylated spirit

Lacking a sense of reality
spattered with wet snow
I walked forward
walked in the four directions
of the world

and that is all
you who are distant close
and alien to me
for all time

Oriole

(from a memoir of Monika Żeromska)

through the half-open door
I gazed at the deep sleep
of an eleven-year-old
whom I did not wish to wake at any price

who could have guessed the child's dreams?
Were they in this world (. . .) or a different one
that adults can no longer see

Have you read the short story "The Oriole"
I'm the oriole
it was for me my father wrote it
for me
and by the way the dedication
you wrote for me in that book
is rather . . . uninspired
banal

whenever I visit you Miss Monika
I'll add
something new
it will be an uncommon dedication
for you I wrote
a poem about a rose

I doubt you read
the last volume of memoirs either Mr. Tadeusz

I confess I've not finished
the most recent volume
the poem about the rose
I wrote for you
so why add a dedication

one day I'll show you poems
and dedications written for me
by the Skamander poets! Tuwim Broniewski Lechoń
even Słonimski

Miss Monika
the Skamandrists were different!
what was it they wrote? *my head's all filled with greenery
and violets grow within*?
my head is filled with puzzlement
and nothing grows within
though sometimes there's a ringing
the Skamandrists were talented grand
somewhat juvenile
they flourished between the two Great Slaughters
cavalry uhlans lances in battle
swords in hand a dream of power
Wieniawa and then Bór-Komorowski

Zawodziński was an uhlan The poems
of Peiper Wat Stern
even Przyboś
seemed suspect to him

Grandfather loved the cavalry
I don't know what he thought about tanks
he maintained order
interned whomever necessary in the camp at Bereza
left and right
I see you have a photo of Grandfather
a warm intimate picture
he's wearing a buttoned dressing gown

at home we referred to the Marshal as "Józwa"
They had a mortal falling out
when *The Coming Spring* appeared

now I've reconciled them
I put these photographs
face to face
I know they loved one another
so let them look each other in the eye

it's February 2002

I'm walking down Stefan Żeromski Street
going to bid farewell to Miss Monika
who has taken her last sleep passed away
I press the button of the intercom
the last name and the first names
Anna Monika written
in green paint

the door opens
an old woman is standing there
she says in a scratchy voice
that no one is in
"and I've got the flu" she adds

the gate slams
I stand for a moment taking in
the building the trees
a magpie caws
the roses are buried
the oriole has flown

Miss Monika's voice
lovely full of life
has faded from the intercom
where are you? come on up
Mr. Tadeusz

I'm at the gate

"I'll let you in"

Broniewski and Gałczyński
used to wait at that gate
after the war
Mama never knew
what to do with them
she'd be on her way to bed

they were so amusing
effusive and tipsy
they sang serenades
actually Broniewski once
got lost in the rain
what am I to do with them
Mama would ask in alarm
both of them were under the influence
Gałczyński disappeared too one time
when I went down to meet them
on the other side of the green gate
there was no one

have you read the short story "The Oriole"
the oriole is me do you like artichokes?
me? I prefer black pudding . . .
artichokes remind me of cactus

where am I to look for you
I don't know where they buried you

I confess
I've not yet finished
that last volume of memoirs

I was in Konstancin
in July 2001
I called you
you had returned from the hospital
seriously weakened

. . .

> "It's past and gone [...]
> Best would be to go mad"
>   (TADEUSZ KONWICKI, *Afterglows*)

And once again
the past begins

best would be to go mad
you're right Tadzio
but our generation doesn't go mad
our eyes stay open
to the very end

we don't need to be blindfolded
we have no use for the paradises
of faiths sects religions

with broken backs
we crawl on

that's right Tadzio at the end
we have to relive everything
from the beginning
you know that as well as I
at times we whisper
all people will be brothers
in life's labyrinth
we encounter

distorted faces of friends
enemies
without name

do you hear me
I'm telling you an image from the past
once again I'm running away
from a specter who
wrapped in a gaberdine of sky
stands in a green meadow
and speaks to me in an unknown language
I am the lord thy god
who led thee out of the house of bondage

everything starts from the beginning

once again Mr. Turski
my singing teacher
looks at me with the handsome
gentle eyes
of Omar Sharif

and I sing
the apple tree has blossomed (...)
red apples did it bear ...
I know I'm out of tune
but Mr. Turski has been smiling
at me since 1930
and I get an A
Mr. Turski in a strange

fragrant cloud
exotic and mysterious
for an elementary school
in a provincial town
between Częstochowa and Piotrków Trybunalski
smiles
and takes his mystery
to the grave

when will the past
finally end

alarm clock

how hard it is to be
the shepherd of the dead

at every step
the living ask me
to write "something" "a few words"
about someone who has died
departed passed away
is resting in peace

and I'm the one who is writing living
living and writing again

let the dead bury their dead

I hear a ticking
it's my old alarm clock
made in the PRC
(*Shanghai – China*)
when the Great Helmsman was still alive
he let a hundred flowers bloom
and challenged a hundred schools of art
to compete
then came the cultural revolution

my alarm clock is like a tractor
it needs to be "wound up with a rake-handle"

(you remember that expression of primitive
pseudo-educated Polish farm managers
"a peasant needs a watch like a hole in the head
he'll only try to wind it up with a rake-handle"
the peasants have forgotten . . . but "the poet remembers")
I wind it up like Gerwazy
the alarm clock wakes me at five
it never fails
it's an old Chinaman nodding his head
in the window of a colonial goods store
above a tin of tea
the alarm clock wakes me several
times a year
reminding me that I have to
travel somewhere fly somewhere
south north
west east
or that I need to rise at dawn
and finish some "poem"
hundert Blumen blühen
(in Munich I bought
Chairman Mao's
little red book
with an introduction
by Lin Biao)

I poet – shepherd of life
have become shepherd of the dead

I have labored too long on the pastures
of your cemeteries Depart now
you dead leave me
in peace

this is a matter for the living

there's a monument

there's a monument
on Ostrów Tumski
melancholy neglected
the monument of the Good Pope

it stands impassive
imperfect (may
God forgive its "creator"
a slip of the hand . . .)

no one lays wreaths here
at times the wind brings
newspapers trash

someone has left an empty
beer can
it rolls across the cobblestones
like metallic
techno music

the wind blows
in the Good Pope's eyes
in his stone ears
across his large nose

no one remembers
who raised it consecrated it
left it

April is the month of remembrance?

on the anniversary of the encyclical
Pacem in terris
I saw a dry stalk
in a bottle
poor Roncalli
poor John XXIII
my pope
he looks like a barrel
like an elephant

they did a number on you

aren't you sad
Holy Father
my dear father

you should rebel
interrupt your sleep
head for Rome
for Sotto il Monte

sleep dream God
and faith alone
stand in Wrocław
a horror in stone

but in my heart
you have
the most lovely monument in the world

I recite for you
poems by Norwid
(according to Michelangelo
Buonarroti)

It's sweet to sleep, but sweeter still to be of stone
In days that shame and calumny have made their own

you smile

you see John you're neglected
because your monument is "wrong"
it was put up by some suspect
organization like Pax or
Caritas with a party affiliation
such were the dark wheelings and dealings
in our country
in yesteryear

you remained yourself you lost none
of your good humor and with your stone
hand jutting from your stomach
as if from a stone cask
you bless me
Tadeusz Juda of Radomsko
of whom it's said
he is an "atheist"

but my Good Pope
what sort of atheist am I

they keep asking me
what I think about God
and I answer
what matters isn't what I think about God
but what God thinks about me

. . .

Master Jakob Böhme
(not my master)

so then
a Silesian shoemaker
by the name of Jakob Böhme
"philosophus teutonicus"
as he was called

who lived by the bridge
in Görlitz

told me how
he saw the gleam of the divine light
in a tin pitcher
or maybe a beer mug

I walked from Zgorzelec to Görlitz
to buy shoes or maybe brandy
armies of ants were marching
over the bridge carrying
Garden Gnomes Gartenzwerge
wicker baskets strong liquor

I've forgotten the details
of the story told by that modest man
and capable artisan

who saw in his kitchen
in some container
the gleam of the absolute

see you descendants in what
modest form God appeared
to the shoemaker of Zgorzelec

(though he was a good shoemaker)

conversation with Herr Scardanelli

(an apocryphal story)

"sehen Sie gnädiger Herr kein Komma"

sehen Sie gnädiger Herr Scardanelli
kein Komma kein Punkt
Doppelpunkt Strichpunkt Gedanken-Strich
and just between ourselves
you were no ordinary madman
you were sometimes the mad Eure Excellenz
sometimes you pretended to be Greek
Leb wohl, Hyperion . . .
Gute Nacht, Diotima . . .

Diotima you dreamed up
from a white glacier
she did not sweat did not eat
lacked that which every maid
and every woman possesses
hadn't a drop of blood in her body
she was a copy of a Greek sculpture
her colors had faded
she was a death mask
poor
poor Scardanelli
the Nazis exploited you
but in *Mein Kampf*
there's not a word about you

Hitler adored Wagner
was himself a character from Kotzebue

Pity you never read
Heidegger's comments
on your poetry
they're brilliant
the professor was a scribbler
wrote indifferent poems
to his Jewish lover
the "lump in pumps"
– as Thomas Bernhard called him –
wanted to be führer to the Führer

I last saw you in Valhalla
near Regensburg
though I didn't see Heine there

you were a thoroughly German
genius and that was why you went mad
later you played the madman
and wrote extraordinary poems from the Tower
Eure Heiligkeit
when you were asked about Goethe
you shrugged
when you were asked about poetry
you shrugged
or you said: "Sehen Sie gnädiger Herr
kein Komma"

[2002]

the poet's other mystery

the poet is 90
and he is 9
and 900

or he is 80
is 8
and is 800

make room for youth
I say to myself
I see
a cat
lying by the fence
its sharp teeth bared
to the sky
little flowers by the stream gazing
with their eyes agleam

the fragrant acacia

I mean I'm not going to start
waking people at night to tell them
that I had good intentions

and I oughtn't to wake my wife
to tell her
I'm afraid of death

it's time to die
but I somehow don't want to
there's one more poem by Leśmian
one more painting by Nowosielski
a sip of red wine
another encounter with Hamlet
I first met him
sixty years ago
he's not changed a bit
I on the other hand

midnight
I read Chekhov smile at him
what a kind good man
he must have loved people . . .
"ich sterbe" he said and passed away

here I have a letter to
Bujnowski
I'll never finish it
because his wife wrote to say
Józek had died
"it's so hard to bid farewell to life" he said
before dying . . .

"Adamaszek" leaves his house
smiles at me
his wife buttons his coat
from his eyes I can tell
he's no idea who I am

though we've known each other fifty years
I can see he doesn't see me
yesterday Mietek called
"Adamaszek died you know"

this morning
I met a mongrel
that I know
sometimes I talk to it
it used to bark at me
it lies in the sun ignoring people
its little muzzle
completely gray

where are you doggy
I know I know you have your own affairs
by the post by the tree
round the corner

The Mystery of the Poetry Reading

From Aristotle
Omne animal post coitum
triste est
praeter gallum, qui post coitum
cantat

at the reading
the poet
rises
and falls with the audience
levitates
drinks water
takes wing

after the reading
by candlelight
or without candles
he takes questions
signs books
writes in journals
receives flowers
kisses a beautiful young lady
on the cheek

flowers ribbons
tied in hair

murmur of voices
the candles are put out
silence

give me your shadow
and your supple neck
no
I don't want shadow

alone in the hotel room

nur narr
nur dichter

throat dry
heart pounding

beneath the candelabras of chestnuts
male and female students
laughing shouting kissing
drinking beer from bottles
standing still
in the moonlight

he hears footsteps
in the hallway
a woman is coming
he hears
another door
closing
the tap of heels

now everything starts again
from the beginning
in a dream
the door opens
he sees
a dress falling
from shoulders
breasts
knees
he wakes
turns on the light
opens *Faust*

I was a man. Then, one dark day I hurled
Blasphemies to myself and to the world.
Today are voices everywhere, such a din
That I no longer know where I can run.

Heart in my mouth, I stand alone in fear.
The door creaks loud, but no one enters here.

after a reading
the poet is sad

[*2001*]

Too Bad

I never finished reading
the "Paradiso" mea culpa
I got bored in the "Purgatorio"
mea culpa
the "Inferno" alone I read
with flushed face
mea maxima culpa

Ezra Pound read not only all of
Dante and Confucius
but also the poet from Predappio
(la Clara a Milano!)
whom he adored

Pound was a madman a genius
and a martyr
His favorite student
Possum
wrote beautiful poems about cats
wore tasteful neckties
and was more temperate in speech
than his master
for which he received the Nobel Prize

Pound
was right
not to be fond
of capitalists and moneylenders

he sought to drive the merchants
from the temple
he was put
in a straightjacket
in this outfit
he roams Parnassus
conversing with the admirer
of Dante Ariosto Schiller
Klopstock Platen
and Weiblinger . . .
with the poet composer leader
translator and author of the poem
Die Worte vom Brot
with Benito Mussolini himself!
(serves you right! you foolish poet)

PS
too bad Pound never finished
Mein Kampf
before he started extolling
the Führer

Done In

Done in
by a plank
on a trash heap Pier Paolo
tries to rise from the dead
crawls

enclosed in his hands he bears
bloody human
genitals like a chick
in the nest
up to the Lord's throne

and this divine earth
with its unearthly beauty
this lesion in the universe
this canker in the loins
of the milky way
spits blood and sperm

it was you Pier Paolo
who said
"Far off a person sees someone
who is killing another person.
He's a witness to the act,
he distances himself from it . . ."

someone
saw from far off
another person
who was killing you
La Terra vista dalla Luna
il porcile
a barely fledged youth
giovane di primo pelo
a kitchen boy with the burning eyes
of La Fornarina
clenching his buttocks
the rectum of paradise

too young for the noose
for a death sentence an amorino
consuming the shit of the world
one of the heroes
of *Salo or 120 Days of Sodom*

Created in the image
and likeness of God
Pier Paolo awaits
the day of judgment

The Philosopher's Secret

ich werde von Zeit zu Zeit
zum Tier – dass kann ich
an nichts denken als an
Essen, Trinken, Schlafen
Furchtbar!

this confession
came in the private diary
of the philosopher

now interpreters publishers
slave traders relatives
have sold
the person

it's the revenge of his
famous assertion
(conjecture?)
Wovon man nicht sprechen kann
darüber muß man schweigen

a saying as common and as hackneyed
as the Mona Lisa's smile
as the tongue Albert Einstein
poked out at the journalists

September 5 1914
I lie on straw – on the ground –
I'm reading and writing
on a small wooden trunk
(preis 2,50 kronen)
wrote the philosopher
today once again I mas ——

things are so tough – wrote the philosopher
Lord take pity on me
I'm a worm
but with God's help I'll become
a person
and he wrote
that he'd have to take his own life

I'm going through hell

Lord may the cup
pass me by
the mind is asleep in the head
wrote
the philosopher
then he wrote that he was afraid

and now bad people
have sold the philosopher
and his great secret
that he mas ——

like a boy or a recruit
like a million a hundred million boys
it's all half-scary half-funny
like the tiger in the circus
or the monkey masturbating
in the zoo
in plain sight
of its larger brothers
from the vanishing species
of *Homo sapiens*

Wittgenstein served as a volunteer
on a ship called the Goplana
it was still sailing
between Kraków and Sandomierz
after the second world war
when I was a student
or maybe I just dreamt it!
the Goplana with its great paddle wheel

Der Wachschiff Goplana

In Krakau
Trakl vor wenigen Tagen
gestorben ist

additional uses for books

large books and small
can be variously utilized

in the morning
upon waking
jump briskly out of bed
(don't waste the day!)
take a book
(if you have one at home)
and begin your exercises

walk in a straight line
with the book
on your head

you ask
"which book"
this isn't about books
it's about balance

place one foot
in front of the other
do not move your hips
from side to side

set the book
aside

"which book?"
it could be *Quo Vadis*
With Fire and Sword
J. R. R. Tolkien
Der Herr der Ringe
(mit Anhängen)
Baudolino
An Ancient Legend
it makes no difference
it could be something shortlisted

walk straight
with eyes closed
stretch out your arms
to the sides
walk in a straight line

take a deep breath

[Wrocław 2002]

why do I write?

sometimes "life" conceals
That
which is greater than life

Sometimes mountains conceal
That
which is beyond the mountains
so the mountains must be moved
but I lack the necessary
technical means
and the strength
and the faith
to move mountains
so you will not see it
ever
I know
and that is why
I write

March 21 2001 – World Poetry Day

around noon the phone rang
"today is poetry day"
said Maria
"I can't hear you!"
"today is World Poetry Day, o poet!
it's been established by Unesco"
Even Ionesco couldn't have thought up
something like this! this is something (something)!

"Poet, I send you
best wishes on your own holiday"
said M. imperturbably
tomorrow is world rheumatism day
I replied and
sat for a moment to
put on my boots . . . damn laces
one end always longer than the other
tangled like the black spaghetti
advertised in Malbork
by charming grandma Zosia from Naples

How did Leopold Staff put it?
Something must be tied,
something joined,
something resolved.

before I'd tied them
the phone rang

"good morning
pardon my boldness
but I'm an old lady
close to death could
I come round right now
and read you my poems?"
no!
I replied gruffly . . .
but I relented . . . (embarrassed)
"how old are you exactly?"
seventy

well I'm eighty
I'm sick
(and I was "half-dead")
but you look so well on the television
your neighbor the lady who runs the steam press
saw you . . . I'm ill too . . .
the voice unwound softly
like a ball of yarn in a dream
sweet painless
"I live round the corner"

I can't
I repeated more quietly
feeling like a killer of old ladies
a butcher (or baker) from the Old Town
a murderer Jack the Ripper Jacques the Fatalist
"my grandson persuaded me to write
and my daughter-in-law to paint" said the old lady
actually old ladies can hardly be blamed

for painting writing poems making cutouts
if ladies in high heels
write novels
compose music
to their own words release records
a golden mask a handprint in Między
zdroje a Fryderyk Prize
after all these women in (or past) the prime
of life could be doing so many other
things . . .

One is in Paris
one is in Naples
the third: Hans Metaphysikus
"in seinem Schreibgemache"
and for me an old lady is waiting
round the corner

my leg hurts
my eye hurts
grauer Star
Geschwulst am linken fuß
gestörter venöser Zirkulation
Ulcus cruris varicosum
gichtischen Schmerzen nehmen zu

In Toledo I bought
Spanische Fliege
eine Tasse Fliegertee
didn't help!

forgive these ostentations
these linguistic flirtations
(I'm doing it for my critics)
Spanish fly is just a compress
or a tincture
from the beetle Lytta vesicatoria
maybe I'll manage
to make my deepest self possessed
by some philosopher
because I make myself depressed
by being too shallow

poet in applesauce

on an endlessly
long
golden honeysweet
strip of
flypaper

in a little blue tux I see
a great medium
small
poet

I see a fly
on the strip
blowing into its blocked proboscis
stretching out a leg
cleaning its sticky
wings
its legs flailing
piping a song: *Root-toot-toot* –
warming up for battle

rubbing its hands

in an empty vodka bottle
it deposits its suffering
(for posterity)

on the milky way I see
a black spitfly
(spitting and apologizing
apologizing and spitting)

after a thunderous flight
a soft landing
on a rubbish bag
in some radical
porno-rag

you hear the heroic buzzing
in space (that's our *Root-toot-toot*
making a face)

him too

him too he writes
poems
Adam!

the spoon raised to his lips
Adam froze

you hear? I'm talking to you
Adam . . . he's not listening!
so then dear friends
Mr. Onufry Mr. Teofil's neighbor
writes too
and he's pretty good
dashing off
all kinds of stuff and nonsense
fairy tales idylls bucolics pastorals
ballads limericks dactyls iambs
historical songs elegies
rhapsodies chivalrous legends
epics comic sagas
hexameters trochees
eat up Adam
or your beet soup
will get cold!

Adam frozen
gave Mr. Onufry
a piercing look

while the latter
thinking that our Bard
had a dumpling from his soup
stuck in his throat
gave Adam such a whack
on the back with his hand . . .
the table grew jollier
right away . . .
Only Mr. Antoni was upset
turning red as a poppy
then the blood drained
from his face and he too froze
the lady of the house swooned
and salts infusions and fans
were set in motion

PS
I'm letting you know, my good Mr. Władysław,
since you asked me to write to you
about your late father, to tell you what I remember
and what I saw with my own eyes, I send this to you
with blessings and greetings . . . and since
you yourself apparently dabble
in writing, perhaps you can explain
the mystery of why the word "too" sometimes
makes such a dramatic impression
on bards . . . because we ordinary mortals
though we scribble our own stuff and nonsense
and little poems, lose neither
our good humor nor our appetite,
something I also wish for you.

a cold in China

I was in China in autumn 1958
a billion Chinese (or maybe half a billion?)
were preparing for the "great leap forward"

in the hallway of the Shanghai hotel
I met a man
with a scarf round his throat
he held a handkerchief to his mouth
indicating with his eyes that he could not speak
his traveling companion
explained to us that the painter Nacht (Samborski)
had a cold a sore throat that he apologized
worried he'd get the flu
afraid of conversation of bacteria
he was steering clear of drafts he apologized
he had a cough and a temperature of 99
he was avoiding all contact was afraid of amoebas
was keeping his mouth closed . . . living on crackers and tea
he intended to interrupt his journey he wasn't
flying to Canton but would return home
he would go to the sanatorium at Laski
afraid to speak
the great artist
and gifted storyteller
took off quickly
without a handshake

Witold Z. stood with gaping
mouth and eyes (still blue
then) wide open
he looked at me
on his
face
there appeared a wordless question
half a billion Chinese were taking
the "great leap forward"
and one little fellow from Warsaw
had a cold and so
was paying no attention
to this minor event
because his cold because his nose because he'd sneezed
bless you
how could this be explained

I smiled toward the painter's back

and right then I took a liking
to Witek Z.
because of his capacity
for surprise

because of his openness

and though in the dining car
from Peking to Shanghai
he was hungry . . .
and was most upset

that I got my lunch first
we're fond of each other
and admire one another
to this day

along the tracks there could be seen
people defecating
facing the train and smiling

in the morning mists the figure
of someone exercising
faded away

every few years
we reminisce not only about the stumbling
"great leap" and the great wall
the black chrysanthemum and the painter
but also
the thoroughly frightened
Polish journalist
the brave and wise
Polish student
the opera and the circus

and also the throng of children around us
laughing and shouting

when asked
what the children were shouting
our interpreter and guide

answered that the children
were exclaiming "long live Chinese-Polish friendship"
but a few days later in a whisper
he explained that they had been saying
"long noses long noses"
we took a closer look at our noses
they were neither long nor short
noses can be funny
and two buttons (behind)? what was it Norwid wrote?
I'll add that when they see us, Chinamen
Are struck above all else by buttons two
Behind – "what are those things," they ask; "explain
Their purpose . . ."

Bad Music

(marginal notes on a music festival)

bad music is the gas
of a defecating demon
Cacophony Caca-making
bad music is sh . . .
on which an idol
in the latest Love Parade
in Berlin its motto
"music is the key"
slipped and broke his leg
participants in the parade
left several tons of trash condoms
and one corpse

producers of bad
music
ought to be
castrated
have their ears cut off
they'll sing small
in hell

retired bearded "idols"
leap about
at funereal festivals
festooned with me-loud-ious
woeful bacchantes

the old jerk recalls
jazz in the catacombs of communist Poland
martyrs in red socks
with tears in his eyes
and hair like St. Genevieve
he bawls
Ilur Ilurv Iluryou

he's accompanied
by an utterly humorless
presenter
the "emcee" who
vomits what he said years back

while the public poor saps
buy the whole ball of wax
with ovations
standing
sitting
and excreting

the spilling of blood

blood
the young blood
of "those years"

diluted by dishwater
and the hatred
of old people
who survived

blood spilled once
for freedom equality independence
for God Honor and Homeland
is now spilled emptily
by two hundred organizations
fighting among themselves
for monuments plaques
awards and cash

old men bearing arrogant
expressions in caps with four
corners like horns
and outsized pants
fighting among themselves
an eye for an eye
a tooth for a tooth

when I listen
to my comrades in arms
as they salute empty foreheads
and
instead of sharing a bowl
of wartime pea soup
drinking a glass
and having a sing (and a fart)
snarl and spit
at one another

when I listen to these hellish squabbles
my own blood boils

Escape of the Two Little Piggies

(from the slaughterhouse death camp)

today someone told me
an amusing and most curious
story . . . it took place
on the isle where the tribe of the Britons
clone sheep where the cow's milk
has the nutritional value of a woman's milk
where people and even dogs
go mad
after consuming meal made of lamb's brain

so these little piggies escaped from the slaughterhouse
they dug a hole under the fence
fled across a field through a wood
swam a stream and a river

guard dogs and helicopters
gave chase on land and sky
while flocks of cloned sheep
stood bleating nearby

till at last the fugitives were caught

now "humanity" came to the rescue
moved by the fate
of God's creatures
and instead of turning the piggies

into hams and pork roasts
the authorities gave them a lifelong
pension The heir to the throne himself
extended his protection to the piggies
upon hearing this news
my dwindling faith in the Prince
returned
newly reborn

PS
three days later I read
that the piggies' lives are in jeopardy
as the slaughterhouse owner has sued
seeking to get his piggies back and make 'em
into trotters and hams
ribs sausage and bacon
(the law is on his side . . . the property laws . . .
and in foggy Albion the law
is a sacred thing) . . .
how the story ended I do not know
as the previous century departed
and the age of Harry Potter started

The Weeping Superpower

(Saturday January 20 2001)

I'm reading Norwid

Across the mobile surfaces of the Sea
A song like a seagull, Jan, to you I send . . .

Long will it fly to the homeland of the free –
Doubting the land will still be there to find? . . .

I'm at a writers' retreat in Konstancin
I'm talking with Kapuściński
about Franek Gil
about globalization
we drink wine
I speak of population growth
he of water shortages
not oil but water
not water
but water shortages will be the cause
of future wars says Ryszard
blood will be spilled for water
not for homeland honor and god

it's gotten late

I hear that far away
in Washington sleet is falling
it's cold lousy weather

the 43rd president of the Superpower
is being sworn in
there's a 21-gun salute at the Capitol

The superpower is sentimental
tender-hearted sensitive
("mitfühlender Konservatismus")
tearful
the "compassionate conservative"
places his hand on the bible
he's the son of the 41st president

Abraham Lincoln watches and listens

even the sleet was unable
to conceal Bush's tears of emotion
the superpower was weeping

the president's wife Laura wept
his twin daughters wept
the president's parents
former president George Bush
and his wife – Grandma Barbara – were weeping
those who voted for Gore wept
after making sloppy holes
in their ballot papers
so the holes had to be recounted
the outgoing president Bill Clinton
wept his wife Hillary wept
(she wept but she took chairs
and an armchair she wept but she took a table

and curtains and some other things
. . . though she gave them back) their daughter
Chelsea was weeping Madeleine wiped her eyes
as she stood there in her miniskirt
with a rose pinned to her bosom
Bronek wept too
(though for different reasons)
the former national
security advisor
Sandy Berger
"kept reaching for his handkerchief"
the sky was weeping
vice-president Dick Cheney
wept as the 43rd president
put his own overcoat round him
to protect him from the rain . . .
(the "compassionate conservative")
then raised his own collar
(to keep the rain from trickling down his neck)

a small unknown intern
wept as did her mother
who was left with a stained dress
in the closet
"my daughter, my little girl". . .
what have you done?!
then there was a grand ball
made of a hundred balls
oh! what a ball it was

the gentlemen were required (?) to wear tails
and cowboy boots
or a tuxedo
and cowboy boots

top hat stetson and cowboy boots

then there was a banquet
seven thousand pounds of beef were consumed
(the old world will feel the effects in a few years
or a few days)
five and a half thousand pounds of ham
(this bodes no good either)
sixty thousand giant shrimp

the former president once again
bid farewell to the nation
once again apologized
to the district attorney and the nation
that he had lied that he had put his finger
where he shouldn't have
the finger from the atomic button
(don't put your finger in the door!)
he promised he'd give back the chairs
and flew off

the sky wept the earth wept
the lands and oceans trembled
diplomats and generals
wiped their noses

(the cardinals smiled)

I wept too
as I read the papers
then I laughed through my tears
as I listened to the radio

building the Tower of Bauble

she would gaze upon her features
innocent and so attractive
in the mirror every morning
and at night before retiring
she would gaze upon her features
oval white
and appetizing
as a slice of bread and butter

once she looked in a pier glass
(an heirloom from an aunt or grandmother)
and saw herself
full length
from head to foot

she turned her head with winsome grace
and she saw her other face
or rather her coin's alternate
side
in the mirror magnified

she gazed upon the face
of an angel
which changed
in eyes mirrors
till many years later
in a star-filled

(one- or maybe four-star) hotel
her eyes to the ceiling directed
found her body reflected
as in a sheet of water

she read "rip van winkle"
noticed that she herself had no
winkle
the pier glass came to mind again
she took another look
sharp wordless and then
after in the bath she sought
herself and her identity
drank Kafka with cream
invoked Potter's assistance
climbed up on Pegasus
and winged in this manner
sat down (on her backside)
to compose an auto
biographical novel
"building the tower of bauble"
her patron was kundera
and the thoughts of Haripoter
Chagall's flying cows
she read the daily lama
dipped into ulysses
found her grandfather's roots
became an unmarried mother
but wrote on like no other

"Building the Tower of Bauble"

on the way for the heck of it
she scribbled some poems
"rose without thorns"
and "thorn with no rose though it grows"

she won prizes
was a huge hit
in magazines you'd find
pictures
of a ravishing
behind

she took an interest in noah's ark

and wrote on like no other

"The Tower of Bauble" has reached the sky
so maybe it's time
to bid it goodbye – she thought –

because it'll make a hole in the sky

or maybe there's still time
to fill the hole with the kama sutra
Adolf Hitler and the brahmaputra
Stalin and bill clinton's finger
all the stops
must be pulled out!
so she knuckles down and buckles down
writing like no other no other
throws it all into the sack

cloning and genes and infestations
wives' and mothers' obligations
and the intern's vestmentations
a great big bang
tummy upset
porno on the internet
c-section and a quadruplet

she writes like no other
writes like no other
all asweat . . .

Mutter fleht: Sandra
bitte stell Dich! . . . and my
mama fukuyama . . . doesn't
get a Thing . . .

exit

. . .

white isn't sad
or happy
just white

I keep
telling it
it's white

but white doesn't listen
it's blind
deaf

it's perfect

and oh so slowly
it becomes
whiter

philosopher's stone

this poem
should be put to sleep

before it starts
to philosophize
before it starts

to cast about
for compliments

summoned to life
in a forgetful moment

attuned to words
to glances
it seeks deliverance
from the philosopher's
stone
passerby walk on
don't lift the stone

under it a tiny white poem
naked
is turning
to ash

[2002–2003]

words

words have been used up
chewed up like gum
by lovely young mouths
have been turned into white
balloons bubbles

diminished by politicians
they're used for whitening
teeth
and for the rinsing out
of mouths

in my childhood
words could be
applied to a wound
could be given
to the one you loved

now
diminished
wrapped in newspaper
they still contaminate still reek
they still hurt

hidden in heads
hidden in hearts
hidden under the gowns

of young women
hidden in holy books
they burst out
they kill

[2004]

landslide

we've been struck by a landslide
of rocks stones pebbles

you could say that the poets
have stoned poetry to death
with words

only the stuttering
Demosthenes made good
use of pebbles
turning them
in his mouth
till he bled
he became one of the greatest
orators
in the world

PS
I too stumbled on a stone
at the very start of my journey

my old Guardian Angel

the avalanche of angels
brought about
by inspired poets
artists priests
and American
movie directors
is infinitely more foolish
than the one brought about
by Romantic poets

the products
of the dream factory
– the "holy wood" –
are sugary white
like the cotton candy
young children
adore

my Guardian Angel who
is 83 years old
and remembers all
my misdeeds
flew to me in consternation
and told me he was
being pestered
by salesmen
pedophiles sodomites

from commercial public
and religious TV
to endorse "angel's milk" custard
with little wings
dance hip-hop with seniors
and sell
sanitary napkins with wings
and without

they gave him
a gold watch with no time
a depilator a vibrator
a cell phone a garden gnome a paid
trip to Babylon

another empty vessel
offered him
the post of Angel of Europe
and guardian angel of the euro

my good old Guardian Angel
hid his face in his wing
and wept
"don't cry" I said –
O heavenly angel guardian mine
Stand beside me all the
time! Morning noon and in the night
always keep me in your sight
from all evil keep me far

at this point my Guardian Devil
flew up on the
black wings
sprouting from his heels

my Guardian Angel and my Guardian Devil
began to fight
for my little soul

golden thoughts against a black background

since awakening
I've been having black thoughts

black thoughts?

try perhaps to describe
their form their substance

how do you know they're black

maybe they're square
or red
or golden

that's it!

golden thoughts

golden flakes in a dead sea
of tired language

those from Gogol for instance
"nothing reassures
like history"
or
"humor is no laughing matter"

and one other thought
that should be contemplated
by young people
and those "in the prime of life"

"it would be a poor world
without old people"

PS
there'd be no one to give your
seat to in the streetcar
and what use is life
without good deeds

à la Wyspiański

in dreams I see a crowd
moving toward me

in dreams
I see ever more people
talking shouting

while in life nothing
rouses me any more

in dreams they speak to me
the dead the living
word after word
falls apart

flowers push in
through empty eyes
earth pushes in
through sockets

I brush off stars with my eyelids
I hear the heart of the bell
crack

I hear Wawel rocking to and fro
putting the nation to sleep

such is the master

he wakes
looks about
something should remain
of the things of this world
but what?

the angels have departed

Tipsy
on sleep on wine
sated with gall
and vinegar
the old poet
strives to remember
which of the things of this world
were supposed to remain

poetry and love
or maybe poetry and goodness
he chews the words toothlessly
goodness I think it was goodness
and beauty?
or perhaps compassion?

he steps back
to better see Warsaw

The other one was beautiful and evil
her "sister" ugly and good

such is the master
playing while he spurns
obscuring so as to explain

he closes his eyes sees two
nailed feet

they fly from the planet

fairy tale

my legs were numb
I woke
from a long
uncomfortable
sleep

into a pure world

into a light
newly born
into Bethlehem or perhaps
another "lowly" town

where no one murdered
children
or cats
or Jews or Palestinians
or water or trees
or air

there was no past
and no future

I held hands
with mommy and daddy
in other words God

and I felt so good
it was as if
I didn't exist

[Christmas 2002]

. . .

Dostoevsky said
if he had to choose
between Jesus and the truth
he would choose Jesus

I'm beginning to understand
Dostoevsky

the birth life death
resurrection of Jesus
are a huge scandal
in the universe

without Jesus
our little planet
is devoid of consequence

this Man
son of God
if he died

rises again
each day at dawn
in anyone
who emulates him

[2003–2004]

finger to the lips

the mouth of truth
is closed

a finger to the lips
tells us
the time has come

for silence

no one will answer
the question
about what truth is

the one who knew
the one who was truth
is gone

the last conversation

instead of answering
my question
you put a finger to your lips

said Jerzy

does it mean
that you won't
that you can't answer

it's my reply
to your question
"what meaning does life possess
if I have to die?"

placing a finger on my lips
I answered you in my thoughts
"life possesses meaning only because
we have to die"

eternal life
life without end
is existence without meaning
light without shadow
echo without sound

. . .

ever since the "little"
pope
smiled at me
the world has been a tad better

lord! What was his name

Luciano
or Luciani
that's it
Albino Luciani

He was like a child
he asked
what had happened
at the Ambrosiano
bank

when that little pope
smiled at the world
the "grown-ups"
took offense

Children would ask him
if they could call
God
mommy and daddy

he answered
yes
yes you can
God may contain
more of the Mother than the Father
(at which Cardinal B. made a face)

Naive as a child
though wise as an owl
he sought to know
the mysteries of banks and accounts
and money laundering
he died of a heart attack

they took some papers from his hands
and gave him a book on Emulating
Jesus
he emulated him well
he tried to drive the merchants from the temple

he left behind some worn slippers
eyeglasses and a smile
that illuminates
our depths

[2001–2002]

heart in mouth

in 1945
in October
I left the resistance

I began to breathe

word by word
I regained speech

it seemed to me
"Everything"
was working out
not only in my mind
but in the world
at home in Poland

along with Przyboś I sought
a place on earth
along with Staff I began
the rebuilding
with the smoke from the hearth
along with Professor Kotarbiński
I voted three times yes

I took a seminar
with Professor Ingarden
introduction to the theory of cognition

Hume helped me
to organize my ideas

the referendum was rigged

the rebuilding of the temple
proceeded in accordance with
the plan and the dream
God left me alone
do what you like you're a grown-up
he said
don't hold my hand
don't turn to me
with every little thing
I have two billion people to worry about
in a moment it'll be ten billion
I helped you in 1935
with those algebra problems
said God
from a burning bush
that turned to ash

the 21st century was sneaking up like a thief

my mind
scattered to the four corners of the earth
on the wall I saw
an inscription Mene Tekel Peres
in Babylon a knife at humanity's throat

poor Stachura the poet

near the unclean channel
of the Vistula
a herd of sows and boars were grazing
alongside Apollo's children

to this cafeteria
there came from a far country
Janko the musician a lad possessed by poetry
he cast pearls before swine
sang played on a golden comb
till he heard voices
and went mad

he was like a butterfly
in a spider web

I talked with him
just one time
at a writers' retreat
he stood in the door
of my room
and asked for a sheet
of paper

I told him I had
only squared
recycled paper

he gave a polite smile
thanked me
and left
with three sheets

sometimes I think he meant
something else

that he meant his and my
and our life

[September 2003]

labyrinths

the leśmianek emerged from the fetal waters
and was entranced by the world

through the hollowing out of the afterworld
through excess and inattention
he became a poet and tumbled
into the labyrinth of God

he sought a way out in language
but language has no way out

he sought more zealously
than any
other Polish poet

then he tried to flee from life
seeking shelter in poetry

but from the labyrinth of life there is
no way out (except via death)

the leśmianek shrank out of despair
and faded away till he died
as an unearthly notary
somewhere in Zamość Hrubieszów
and Częstochowa

as a reward for his unavailing faith
he was transformed
by the radiant god
of poets
into a garden gnome

in a cap of invisibility
with a runny nose
beneath a broad viburnum leaf
he waits for the end of the world
the end of history
the end of the end

but the world refuses
to end

[January–February 2003]

Ashurbanipal killing a wounded lion

it is an unutterably beautiful
bas-relief
– *From the Palace of Ashurbanipal at Nineveh* –

what dignity and mutual respect there was
in encounters between beasts and humans
before firearms were invented

I always stand hushed
before this scene
the king of the beasts
and the king of slaves
in a mortal embrace

Calm on the face
of Ashurbanipal

a grimace of pain and rage
on the lion's muzzle hidden in its mane

the King's beard artfully dressed
his face saying I am the king of the world
king of beasts and humans
king of earth water air
king of kings

the sword transfixes the animal

the lion pierced by fletched
arrows
the king clad in a robe
and plates of armor

locked in their mortal embrace
they remain distant

Their encounter will be won by the side
that wielded the sword
the lance the bow
extensions of the arm
technology
intelligence or in other words
subterfuge

perhaps that is why the lion
is condemned
to perish

while the human species
has filled the earth

eternal return . . .

Nietzsche is back in fashion
he's returning to Germany (and Poland)
indirectly
via Paris
in the guise of a French philosopher
of Romanian extraction

this Zarathustra of Naumburg
part Polish gentleman
part Übermensch

asks himself
his mother
his sister

why am I so wise
bold unique crucified

don't trouble your head over it
counsels his mother
concentrate on those Greeks of yours
or compose something

His sister "liebes Lama"
is just back from South America
she's a little anxious but proud
that her brother stands straight

and looks like a soldier ("fast")
"auch Magen und Unterlieb in Ordnung"

Fritz left for the train station
carrying flowers but without the big sword
that he took to the photographer's
and to the war (as a stretcher bearer)

then as befits an eagle
he sought out an eyrie
in Genoa and environs
"sono contento"
he wrote home

the good residents of Genoa
call him "il piccolo santo"
"il santo"
has regretfully given up
the notion of eternal return
he makes himself risotto macaroni
(without onion or garlic)
tomatoes artichokes with egg
diet is the essence of philosophy
what one eats is expelled
in the form of thought
"die ewige Wiederkunft"

he asked his mother what
"ordinary" "simple" people eat
what our poor eat

"solitary Nietzsche"
did not know "simple" people
had not encountered poverty

our people
dear Fritz
from morning to night eat potatoes
fatty meat
pigmeat
wash it down with schnapps
and drink a catlap
they call coffee

oh! Mama
just an endless round of pork
potatoes catlap
sauerkraut?

how little I know our nation
I've always eaten alone

but it's all the fault
of the Social Democratic leaders
Mama . . .
a man ought to be
brought up for a soldier
a woman for a soldier's wife

with tears in his eyes
he parted company with the idea

of eternal return
understanding
that eternal returns to Naumburg
are nothing special

the climate was "wrong" and the food
and the neighbors
and his sister Lama and his mother
however dear she was . . .
and his aunts!
can an eagle have aunts?
even if they're kind and affectionate

"das Meer liegt bleich
und glänzend da
es kann nicht reden"

philosophers

"Das Wesen der Wahrheit
Ist die Freiheit"
wrote Martin Heidegger
in 1930
then he joined
the Nazi party
"Hampelmann der Nazis"
he was called
by the righteous among philosophers
Karl Jaspers

but he too was wrong
when he told Hannah Arendt
who was frightened by Hitler's victory
"Das Ganze ist eine Operette
Ich will kein Held in einer Operette sein"
H. A. emigrated . . .
and he and Gertrude
his Jewish wife
realized
that this was no operetta

a crystal night fell
on Germany and on Europe
the starry sky dimmed
the moral law died

what Aquinas saw

a note in the margin
of an article by Father Tadeusz Bartoś
"The Curious World
of Thomas Aquinas"

on December 6 1273
during mass he has an experience
that makes him give up writing
"I cannot write any longer,
I have seen things next to which
all my writings are as straw"

What did Aquinas see?
"I have seen things" he said
and stopped speaking

what things?

Aquinas did not understand
women children or art
– so they say – maybe he was afraid
maybe he didn't want to understand

"I have seen things"

maybe he saw a woman angel
giving birth to a child

a god and redeemer
maybe he saw God
the Father and the Mother

maybe he saw
a woman priest
smiling at him
flirtatiously

maybe he saw his own
conception and birth

and understood that woman
is not a mistake of nature
but is nature itself

through Aristotle I feel
a certain indistinct connection
with this Father of the Church

I'm impressed by the weight
of his flesh spirit and reason

he reminds me physically
of Doctor Martin Luther

this breed of hippopotamuses
brought gravity back to the Church

I see their huge bodies
immersed
in the living water
of faith hope and love

[January 31 2003]

learning to walk

"langgestreckt auf meiner Pritsche
starre ich auf die graue Wand"

for the last two years I've been taking lessons
from Pastor Dietrich Bonhoeffer
who was hanged
on April 9 1945

at the order of the Führer
Hitler Hiedler Hüttler
Hitler Schickelgruber
or whatever his name was

The Führer croaked on April 30
with his faithful dog
(poor dog)

in my long life
I've taken lessons not from poets alone

from Goethe Hölderlin Heine
Rilke
"Denn das Schöne ist nichts
als des Schrecklichen Anfang (...)"

Rilke to the end of his life
clung desperately

to women's gowns
hiding in the folds of their skirts
till the day he died
he wore the girl's frock
in which his mother
had dressed him

"she was like a gown
ghastly and terrifying"

if he had only stayed for a moment
with Heinrich Ziell
Am Pferdefleischwagen!
But Rilke chose the angel's tower
chose the Princess of Thurn und Taxis
so I left him and went to seek
instruction from Brecht
on the way I met Grabbe
(extraordinary fellow!) and Benn

Bonhoeffer I met in Wrocław

start from the beginning
start again he would say to me
learn to walk
learn to write to read
to think

you must accept the fact
that God has gone from this world

he isn't dead!
you have to accept the fact
that you're an adult
that you have to live
without a Father

and he also said
that you have to live with dignity
in a godless world
without counting on punishments or rewards

did I not sin
comparing the Führer
to a dog? after all he was a man
he had a mother and father
a sister and brother
he was an artist he left
watercolors and drawings
he was a writer he loved Wagner
he left "Mein Kampf"
there are rumors in my country
that "Mein Kampf" has been published
in Polish but no one
has seen or heard anything . . .
alas the Führer croaked
and the Jewish problem still awaits
its final solution
"Endlösung der Judenfrage"

Jews Arabs Poles and Germans
are a little oversensitive
everywhere they detect antisemitism
and yet the forest of trees
planted by the hands of the Righteous
grows green thickens
rises to the windows of our
homes
there are excellent comedies
about Auschwitz Majdanek Sobibor
the Passion and the Holocaust are becoming
ever more profitable
four hundred million dollars is serious money
not a mere thirty pieces of silver

we sat in the shade of trees
in a small beer garden near
St. Elizabeth's

Bonhoeffer read me
the poems he wrote in Tegel

"langgestreckt auf meiner Pritsche
starre ich auf die graue Wand"

I gazed at the Light at his monument
that has no head no arms

what if God has taken fright
and abandoned the Earth?

instead of answering
my question
he put his finger to his lips

does it mean
that you won't that you can't
answer my question

wrapped in a stinking blanket
his eyes closed
he listened to the gray wall of his cell
with the eyes of his imagination
he painted it in wildflowers
cornflowers marigolds chamomiles
poppies and more cornflowers
the eyes and lips of his betrothed

those departing footsteps were they hers
or the steps of a condemned
Brother

the slamming of a door

"Ich gehe mit dir Bruder
an jenen Ort
und ich höre dein letztes Wort"

are you refusing
to answer my question
I asked him a second and third time

then he raised his eyes to me
again placed his finger
on his lips

stood up and left

followed Christ
emulated Christ

he walked across a field with other
students hungry they picked
ripe ears of corn
husked the grains ate them
from their hands
they husked the grains with their fingers
I tried to catch up with them
and found myself suddenly in the light
in the land of childhood
in an earthly paradise I recovered
the eyes and lips
of my girl and cornflowers
and clouds

then He came to a stop
and said
friend
strike out one "big word"
from your poem
strike out the word "beauty"

[Wrocław 2002–2004]

Der Zauberer The Magician

the German papers reported
"Berlin in Christo-Fieber"

Christo swathed the Reichstag
in thousands of yards
of marvelous silver
fabric

first to disappear was the doorway
with the inscription
"Dem deutschen Volke"
"To the German nation"

Once long long ago
before Christo and Jeanne-Claude
were born
the Reichstag went up in flames
the glow filled the sky over Germany
over Europe
over the world
then Heine Brecht
the Mann brothers
were burned at the stake
Benn searched feverishly
for his Aryan roots
Ernst Jünger pulled on his gloves

Goebbels barked
lied through his teeth
he had an artistic soul
wrote plays

Göring guffawed and bellowed
plundered
masterpieces of painting
a fake Vermeer
and a genuine Vermeer

carpet bombing turned
the city to rubble and ash
Adelheid hat Supp' gekocht
die ganze Woch'
auf einem Knoch'
years passed wars passed
the rain stopped falling
the sun rose over Berlin
the smiling end of the 20th century
no one remembered
Lubbe or Dymitrov
it was 1995

the Reichstag wrapped in silver cloth
had forgotten its own history

cold tongues of fire tried to tell
the young about those black flames

but they weren't listening
they were busy with the love parade
with pearls in their belly buttons with earrings

but let's return
to the wrapping of the Reichstag

perhaps it was a symbolic day
marking the marriage
of a historic building
with the present

Chancelor Kohl didn't understand
the point of all the wrapping
he can be forgiven
by accident he became a Historic Figure
chancelor of a united Germany
along with Reagan Wałęsa
he caused the downfall of the empire of evil
helped to bring down the Berlin wall
and the Chinese wall
and to replace the iron curtain
with a velvet curtain

Ernst Jünger removed his gloves

went back to his collection
of butterflies and beetles
turned 100

he left
many books
notes from the Caucasus
from 1942–1943

"yet the partisans are excluded
from the rules of war, if such a thing
can still be spoken of. One encircles them
in the forest like a pack of wolves in order
to destroy them. I have heard things
that belong in the realm of zoology"

he was by disposition an entomologist

we had something in common
I like beetles and butterflies and insects
I fought as a partisan and I am a writer . . .

luxury

Tuesday April 23
the 113th day of 2002

today
I have the day off

I listen to the rain falling
I read poems
by Staff and Tuwim

"I'll be the leading Futurist in the land.
Which doesn't mean I'll be the kind of ass
Who scoffs at poems, and makes a lot of fuss
And plays the magus . . ."

I read a page from the calendar
Angelica
a highly aromatic plant
known to antiquity
can a person recall
the taste of life
the taste of angelica vodka

I listen to the rain falling

such a luxury is
beyond the reach
of the mighty of this world

they have to shake innumerable
sweaty hands kiss flags
pat children
and old crones on the head
wipe their suits and their faces
wipe
paint from their faces
I pity
the "great" (of this world)
because they cannot throw
tomatoes at anyone
they cannot catch
little brats
by the ear

I thank the Lord
I don't have to solicit the votes
of idiots

I listen to the rain

so little
is needed
for happiness

[April 2002–July 2003]

July 14 2004 – in the night

from nature I drew
the bud
of a tea rose
nestling
in green leaves

I had
a green ballpoint pen
and a blue crayon
the flower is blue
and the leaves are green

on July 1 2004 in the newspaper
I had seen blue roses
(along with a caption)

"the Japanese scientists' success
is the fruit of 14 years' work
at a cost of 28 million dollars"

the green leaves surround
both the flowers and the smiling
face of a young woman
a gene from pansies
gave the petals their hue

did those worthy Japanese researchers
with their 28 million "greenbacks"
make something beautiful and useful?
my rose was created from want
theirs from excess and a desire for profit

Such things should not be done
to roses in the land of cherry blossoms . . .

render unto the pansy that which is the pansy's
and to the rose (that) which is the rose's
you are requested to do so
by Tadeusz Rose-wicz poet of Poland

As he walks through the Japanese garden
in the city of Wrocław
he dreams he is in Kyoto
he's done so for half a century

as a young man
he longed to lay a red rose
on the white bosom
of a Japanese woman
at the rising of the sun

before an unknown woman

what extraordinary eyes
enwrapped in shadow
far-away
wide-awake alert
enwrapped in sleep
everything in that gaze is
secret the dusk and the mystery
of her gender and stifled
cries and sighs throbbing
in her white neck

we sit side by side
distance grows and a smile
that fades on its way to me
he's a bit scruffy (funny old man)
absent-minded (he's lost his glasses)
he writes poems
but I'm an old
catcher of butterflies
and of those whose name is frailty
even as a child and a youth
on my fingertips I had
dust from the blue wings
of the eternally feminine

I caught your somewhat
amused smile

and your glance
like a chip of ice
like white-hot
iron

I know
you're like the wildflowers
of my idyllic youth
cornflowers poppies
the distant field
floats away with us
eyes closed

in a guesthouse

a church tower rising
against a clear sky

beyond it a dark blue mountain
woven with the white of birches

today there's not a cloud
to be seen
said Mrs. Jadzia
in a voice that rang
like an invocation
to life
the night phantom melted away
(was that you calling out
in your sleep sir?)

I ate breakfast
signed two books
for some young people
from Krotoszyn
shouted "thank you"
toward the kitchen
locked myself in "my" room
took Geriavit
Concor Proscar Horzol
Rutinoscorbin
primrose extract Bilobil

Vitamin A + E
Espumisan etc

"don't forget your medications"

I sat down at the table

on it (covered
with a newspaper just in case)
lay a long poem
or rather the ghost of one
"gray zone"

I raised my eyes to heaven
saw the ceiling
remembered
the Lacrimal

on the windowsill
were yellow buttercups
or maybe marsh marigolds
Butterblumen
(butter flowers?
or flowers of butter?)

the news
in the papers was filled with blood
everything had become
dark fragile

once again
in the eyes of women
there was fear

the next day I left

letter in green ink

letters arrive

I'm leaving today
(not on Friday)

sending you kisses
thinking of you
missing you
yearning for you

The end of "Operations"
the end of the stay
the end of the innocent
and not-so-innocent flirtations
of the "rut"
under the benches
empty liquor bottles
colored and clear
cheerful blown-up
condoms floating off
balloons balloons
cries the hawker

"throw that in the trash"
I can't throw "that" away
it's your letter
written

in green ink
I can't throw love
in the trash

the sadness of departures
packing the suitcase
the last walk
the last sip of mineral water

I take a souvenir picture
by the old pump room

I pass elderly ladies
three of them
their thinning hair
purple silver red
the last the most fashionable these days
under the "dictatorship of the hairstylists"

in my youth
ladies of that age were called
better halves matrons old dears
caught in webs of wrinkles
painted and beribboned

I stand on the footbridge

I throw into the stream
pieces of the letter
the words "lots of kisses"

"thinking of you"
the white scraps drift away
disappear
the sun sets slowly
the water reddens
I talk to the stream
the stream is never heard
it will never speak
will never utter
the Word

[Kudowa Zdrój 1989]

tempus fugit

    (a story)

A cold coming we had of it
Just the worst time of the year
for a journey, and such a long journey
And the night-fires going out, and the lack of shelters
and the cities hostile and the towns unfriendly
and the villages dirty and charging high prices . . .
"were we led all that way for
Birth or Death?"

Brother Richard's retreat
on the heights
of the fifth floor
is hewn from the slopes of Mount Concrete
outside the window the Akerman Steppe
a thousand hearths
flaring and dying down

Brother Richard's retreat
is inaccessible to clowns
to a certain
species of writers "lady artists"

before the end of the world
Brother Piotr and I are making a pilgrimage
to Akerman Mountain
mors certa hora incerta

this year we were accompanied
by Caspar Melchior and Balthasar
but our ways parted
on Boniface Street (named after a pope?)

We pass Caucasus Street send our greetings
to Prometheus
we wander the labyrinth of roads
at last we reach the place
of magic
(all places in this land are magical)

in a mechanical basket
an invisible power sweeps us
to the eighth floor
we drop to the fifth
in the meantime this fateful force
had transformed us regular joes
into angels (fake ones of course)

often in our journey
we stray
often the impure force casts
us down to the first floor
to the basement even the laundry room
we ask the natives
about the retreat of the elder
Zossima "no one by that name lives here"
they answer in their Mazovian burr
and do you happen to know

which floor Professor
Ryszard Przybylski lives on
they look at us and say
"never heard of him"

after a while we stand
in front of a grille

the grille rises and we are inside
death cell no. 20
which (like a slab of honey)
is fashioned from thousands of books
we smile say nothing
un-eloquently

Ryszard cups his hand
round his ear speak louder
since yesterday my hearing's been de-teriorating

we exchange a few indifferent
words on the subject of angels
which as "subtle beings" were incorporated
into the pictures of Master Jerzy of Kraków
several such subtle beings
hover about Brother Ryszard's head
when he sleeps his un-easy sleep

brother you slept through the birth
of a new Guardian Angel
the Holy Angel of Poland

I see surprise dis-belief
on Ryszard's face
a monument has already been designed
there's a foundation a nomination a jury
things got so silent you could hear a pin drop

Fallen
angels
are like
flakes of soot
like abacuses
like cabbage leaves stuffed
with black rice
and they are like hail
painted red
like heavenly fire
with yellow tongues

fallen angels
are like
ants
like moons squeezing under
the green fingernails of the dead

angels in heaven
are like the inner thighs
of a little girl

they are like stars
shining in intimate places

pure as triangles and circles
inside they possess
tranquility

fallen angels
are like the open windows of a charnel-house
like cows' eyes
like birds' skeletons
like falling airplanes
like flies on the lungs of fallen soldiers
like torrents of autumn rain
that the mouth links to the departure of birds

a million angels
roam
across a woman's hands

they have no navel
they write on sewing machines
composing long poems in the form
of white sails

their bodies can be grafted
onto an olive bough

they sleep on the ceiling
they fall drop by drop

In cell no. 20
I'm the most senior of the condemned

I've been inside for 83 years (like
all the living I've been put away
for life) – with no prospect of
eternity I stare at the ceiling

Ryszard and Piotr are silent
how old are you Rysio? I lead off
Piotr is getting on too
he must be over six-ty?
I'm 69 says Piotr
69 is a magic number
and even an erotic
position

Piotr uses a cell phone a computer a virus
he's the only one who
runs an auto-mobile
and also the Poza Theater
Piotr says worriedly
that Hoene-Wroński has sold Absolut
to some Frenchman

I gaze at the spines
of the books (Mandelstam Lévinas . . .)

slowly book after book
opens
Piotr says to Ryszard
"you know, Tadeusz told me today –
in confidence – that Copernicus' theory

wasn't just harmful for
the church, because people
lived on a flat and motionless Earth
and were happy
the revolutions of heavenly bodies need only
be known to a select group . . . of priests and politicians"
Here I broke in
please don't tell this to Marysia
or to Hania or Jola or Ania . . . for me
the Earth was and is the center of the Universe
humans are the only creatures
who created God who created
humans

Ryszard cupped his hand round his ear
and whispered

"a monk who counted the number of beans
he'd eaten during the day, though he dreamed
of quickly becoming an angel,
deep down was concerned with his body . . ."
I shifted uneasily
in "Vršac Elegy" written for
the poet Vasco Popa I had said
"let's go to dinner I like bean soup"

but Vasco died
and Yugoslavia was dismembered
the eyes of Orthodox icons
were once again gouged out

on Kosovo Polje
broad beans and French beans are
my favorites I've eaten many a bowl
of broad beans with Master Jerzy
. . . *fasolka po bretońsku* soup . . . a treat
from our youth . . .
youth give me wings
and I shall fly above the lifeless earth
together young friends!

Ryszard and Piotr looked
at each other and at me

I am he is you you are me (Lévinas is repeating on me!)
I started to talk with Rysio
about Mandelstam and Nadezhda
about Anna Akhmatova about the transit
camp of Vtoraya Rechka
I climbed on my hobby horse
spoke about Dostoevsky
about the acquittal of Vera Zasulich
about Semyonov Square
and how last year I had visited
Oreshek Fortress
and Walerian Łukasiński's cell

red wine appeared on the table
bread cheese I asked for water
in vino veritas in aqua sanitas
in wine is truth in water is health

I began attacking Lévinas
who's becoming "fashionable". . . I was
annoyed. . . that he took away my
"faces" (a matter still to be cleared up)

Piotr knows what this is about and even
what it's round-about

We fell silent after the silence
Piotr described a scene
that was "played out"
many years ago
in a Parisian café
between Jarosław Iwaszkiewicz
and an unknown woman
who was sitting alone
at a table and weeping
no one was paying any attention
to this "occurrence"
it may have been a fashionable
café frequented by existentialists
by members of the "resistance" (ha ha!)
by collaborators
the woman wept
without hiding her face

Jarosław stood up
crossed to the woman
leaned over her
whispered something in her ear
put his arm round her and kept talking

the woman stopped crying
wiped her tears left

Jarosław returned to his seat
and said (to Piotr)

"when someone's crying
sometimes they need
to be touched held"

We each drank a glass
of red wine

remember – began Ryszard –
how Nietzsche put his arm
round the neck of a cabdriver's horse
and burst into tears? . . . was that in Trieste?

It was in Turin
and it wasn't quite like that
the cabbie was beating the horse about the head
Nietzsche embraced the suffering creature
and wept
wenige Augenblicke später
taumelte er von einem Gehirnschlag gerührt,
zu Boden
Nietzsche knew that the horse
would not utter platitudes
would not console

the superman and philosopher
sought consolation from a horse
and not from Plato
Ryszard says: what are you two laughing at?
Nieztsche went mad but what
became of the horse?
I know . . . the horse
was eaten by the Italians they
eat Polish horses and even
larks (I wrote about it in my play
"Spaghetti and the Sword") they need to be
converted . . . all of them . . .
Moscow . . . Rome . . . Paris . . .

we were supposed to be talking about God
I reminded them

do you know what Mickiewicz said
to a French writer
who invited him to his salon
for conversations about God?

"I don't discuss God over tea"

surely that's a lot wiser than
Nieztsche's dictum "God is dead"
or Dostoevsky's "if there is no God
everything is permissible"

Hora est . . . we were told by Quiet

I'll return the Lévinas
before I leave for Warsaw

God is fashionable Also fashionable is Absolut
God is invited to appear on television
the God of Lévinas the God of Buber
the God of Hegel Pascal Bloch
Heidegger Rosenzweig
he's on between an Argentinean soap coffee and tea

Lévinas thinks that God
can be inflected like a noun
they've turned theology into grammar

Lévinas!
Lévinas learns that he must die
from Jankelevitsch
if God exists philosophy is unnecessary
the philosophy of Heidegger and Rosenzweig

Hora est . . . silence set in
(there'll be no continuation)

but Piotr stirred the waters
and quoted Hegel in a whisper
in German . . .

"es ist der Schmerz, der sich
also das harte Wort ausspricht
daß Gott gestorben ist"

*[Konstancin–Wrocław
January–March 2004]*

knowledge

cogito and dubito
share a house you know
mr cogito above
mr dubito below

having lived a rich life
they switched you know
dubito above
cogito below

both of us are old
and we're aware
for some unknown reason
that we have to die

we're also aware
that the shortest road to the Lord
is Hard Times

as the saying has it
when times are hard folk turn to the Lord

searching for keys

Lord! I left the keys
to the Heavenly Kingdom
in my car

cries a young priest
who lacks a calling
but has good intentions

someone opens up anew
but looks for roots

though a wise old Jew
who sought to be a German
said that humans
have legs not roots

the third lady of Polish theater and film
is searching for her identity
but she can't find the key
to herself
because she left it with the first husband
of the second lady who wrote a book

another lady is searching for the key
out of herself and cannot
find it at home
so she flies to Tibet

as if she couldn't satisfy
this minor need
in Pińczów

a "likeable home-bird"
(as the small ad said)
is searching for her key
in the handbag of a mature lady
with house and car
and "independent" (sic!) garden
she may be a well-padded
Catholic

the merry wives of Warsaw
are turning into
miss-sticks
they jabber away like coffee mills
that have to be from Tibet (etc.)

conversation between father and son
about killing time

poor B. B. said
before he died
"Und nach uns wird kommen
nichts Nennenswerts"

I don't get it, Daddy!

Learn German, son
it'll come in useful
Zeit ist Geld!
Time is money

So why do people
kill their time?

Because when they have time
they get bored, son!

I get bored too, Daddy!

We all get bored
children get bored
and grownups get bored too

Grownup to what, Daddy?

That no one knows

But soccer fans don't get bored?

They get bored too . . .
because the ball isn't round
the match is sold
the ref is bought
you're too young
to remember
the historic goal
that Lato scored
thirty years ago
it was under Gierek
Grandma's always talking about Gierek
and singing
"Under Gomułka we had curds and whey
Under Gierek, meat by the tray
But not a sausage in Kania's day"

Who was Kanyass?
Don't be so curious son
or you'll end up in a barrel of
sauerkraut like those quintuplets
that have been served up for us
for months now by public or religious
or commercial or private television like some
kind of benefit or music festival

But soccer fans don't get bored, Daddy!

Soccer fans go about in facepaint
like cannibals
with sticks knives axes
chains clubs flags
toilet paper
which was in short supply under communism
here and in the evil empire too
but don't forget that Poland
beat Greece though it never became
the Trojan Horse of the European Championship!

Daddy! Is it true that there are players
who don't respect the ball though they're
brilliant and that the philosophy of soccer
has replaced basic theology
and that in Argentina people pray
to Saint Maradonna

Yes son! the light of the goalmouth
has replaced the light everlasting

Drink milk! it'll make you
strong as a Tiger great as Kiepura
or as Rinaldo-Ronaldini!
or as Longinus Podbipięta!

I don't want any milk!

Then eat your custard
and knock it
off!

Daddy! Then I'll be a firefighter!
because firefighters don't get bored!
and when they do they set fire
to forests meadows buildings
even lakes
then they put them out
and are given medals even though
the fires kill off frogs moles
earthworms

Drink some Polish buttermilk son
and stop pestering your father!

Who am I supposed to pester?
Pester your Grandma

Daddy, what's a pedophile?

Eat your angel's milk custard
and leave me alone
will you! Can't you see
that I'm busy and don't have
time to read even
one book by Mendoza
you're an unwanted child
so shut it

Then why did you make me, Daddy,
and how am I supposed to shut it?

children aren't "made"
children are summoned
to life
in unprotected intercourse
Your grandfather used to say
"Have bees, and you'll have honey as well
Have kids, and all your house will smell"
Grandpa's as wise as Fukuyama

Then why don't you bring him home
from the hospital . . . ?!

(not to be continued)

[2004]

we're building bridges

many many years ago
Sister Elisabeth and I strolled
from Zgorzelec to Görlitz
and back
to visit the house of Böhme the shoemaker
to buy thread
drink a Franziskaner Weissbier
learn something about the Rosicrucians
and see a lily in bloom

over the bridge of reconciliation and peace
from dawn till dusk there came
unemployed Polish ants
and retired German ants
the ants were carrying
Europe's Largest Gartenzwergen
Garden Gnomes wicker baskets
quail and ostrich eggs
clothes cabbage asparagus
beer beer beer
bier bier bier
brandy
in the crowd I encountered
mysterious individuals
who winked at me
and offered marks from the time
of Erich Honecker and Helmut Kohl

medals of Soviet heroes
Nikita's pants pieces of the Berlin Wall
they tried to sell me knockoff Absolut
mixed with godknowswhat
by the roads highways
Lechites sat selling berries and
pfefferling mushrooms to the Germans
there were Polish plaster storks
willows wept under the burden
of Polish pears
and Chopin
was left hanging in the wind

there were maidens from the lands of central
and eastern Europe Bulgarians Ukrainians
Russians Poles blondes
qualifying heats for the miss
wet tee-shirt and miss world
competitions were taking place
in the nearby bushes

in the Mona Lisa bar woolen caps and black
tights were being pulled over heads side arms
and firearms cleaned
foundations were established there were no
bathrooms
the former
"leader of the nation" had lost his mustache
the workers their socks
a Polish Raskolnikov

instead of an old money lender
killed a professor
who had flunked him
the "Angel" was gone so was Boniek
Moniek who used to have a clothes shop
had flown away with a stork to
the Promised Land the Roma bought up
all the free plots in the cemetery
where I'd intended to organize
(for myself) a "Polish-style funeral"

you can't scare me

(written on Fat Thursday,
the day after Ash Wednesday, 2002)

young women in Germany
have been hunting men
(with scissors)
cutting off their
ties
at the neck
this practice symbolizes
the taking of power
one staunch lady
cut something more
off her husband
Bild carried
an article
with numerous pictures
the husband however got
to the hospital in time
and the severed tie
penis was sewn back in
place
wife husband and surgeon
are collaborating on
a movie script
a stage play
a bestseller
for a million

in France on Fat Thursday
the ladies don't cut anything off
"on the other hand" everyone eats pancakes
in Poland (on Fat Thursday)
the ladies eat lots of doughnuts
"with rum or without
but with jam . . . I eat them I mama
in other words grandma and daughter"

our ladies don't cut
anything off then sew it
back on again maybe that's why
they find
so many husbands
in the Federal Republic of Germany
in Australia Africa America
and various emirates
maybe that's how Madame Walewska
and Princess Łowicka
along with Marquis Wielopolski
influenced the shape of the Duchy of Warsaw
and the Congress Kingdom

On Fat Thursday
I also heard on the radio
that Osama bin Laden
is very thin
and is six feet tall
that by mistake
in Afghanistan the Americans bombed

British soldiers and a wedding party
and a Chinese restaurant in Belgrade
I'm worried that as part of their
maneuvers they might bomb
the caves in Ojców
led by false information
that it's the hiding place
of King Władysław the Short
about whom the see eye eh and eff bee eye
have been wrongly informed
(by Polish counterintelligence)
that he is only three
feet (tall) lentils are ground
by the mill near the mound
of Krakus and Wanda
I'm overcome with lenten
and unlenten thoughts
that Fat Thursday is followed
by Lean Friday
and lean backsides are followed
by men's eyes

yet

will we find
a remedy for this
before the end of history?!
because
it turns out that between
a chimpanzee and

a
hyu-
man
there's only 1.02%
genetic difference
wow! wau?

I rub my eyes

I wake in the morning
in some jailhouse
without bars

where am I I ask
just where am I

I spot a newspaper on a hook
I see from the language
that it's a Polish paper
our Poland
still unsold
not yet in the hands of Fortinbras
the Norwegian lord

I rub my eyes
where am I
just where am I
I see bars everywhere
this world
is out of shape

someone whispers to me
that it's the kingdom of Denmark

but from the heavens I hear
a song by Moniuszko

Jontek's aria
for bread good sir for bread

so it's not Denmark
I'm in Poland
on Promień Street
thank the Lord!
and where's Napoleon?
Napoleon is with us!
and Chirac? Chirac's without us
in St. Petersburg
maybe he'll meet Telimena there
Master Tadeusz Ryvin Robak
Telimena will explain it all to him

the good Frenchman
was bathed in tears
at the pillory in the Wrocław market square
by the fountain
his hands kissed
by Polish matrons
perhaps he'll forgive us
eat bigos and truffles
wash down his snails with Bison Brand vodka
and his lapin with Chopin
or Polish moonshine
at the world's fair

I wake up there are bars again
I rub my eyes
this world is out of shape

you're at home
you're in your home
in Poland
that is to say nowhere
King Ubu
growls at me
his back turned

so this isn't Denmark

I pull the bars aside! I see a bosom
the bosom of Emilia Plater
and that of Sofia Loren what's she doing
here? advertising noodles
pizza and spaghetti the enchanting
Neapolitanness
she's not the only one promoting us
the great Sam Domingo
will sing to us
out of the goodness of his heart
he won't take a penny
so once again we are
the inspiration of Europe of the World
I hear the flutter of hussars' wings
it's our painted uhlans
flying off to Babylon
and the storks? our storks
have also flown away scared off
by Dutch women what about the nightingales?

though the nightingales have been disturbed
they've remained in the Homeland!

so it's not Holland!
I'm in Poland in Wrocław
in Biskupin on my good
old sofa
I wake in surprise
so we're a kingdom again?
yes yes
the kingdom of two nations!
but the Lithuanians won't have us
Jagiełło's been declared a traitor
they worship Mendog
so what? Landsbergis loves us
plays the piano in the Polish
parliament
a fine Lithuanian even though
he's a nationalist
and Klaus? he sort of looks askance

then what of the Triangle? the Vyšehrad one
it's missing an angle
thank the lord
we have the Weimar triangle
in reserve

our admiral was given
a warship (admiral?
was that Father Jankowski?
why does a priest need a warship

with no cannon no anchor no purpose)
in our department there was
a kind old woman the one
in the miniskirt with the rose pinned to her breast
a big fan of Bronek
when she spoke about Poland
she was in seventh heaven

The Russian tsar is back in Petersburg
a hero
bloody Nikolai
the martyr

the Prussian king
Frederick the Great
has also returned
to his plinth in Berlin

the Bulgarian king is back
the Romanian king
the prince of Paris
and also our good emperor
and apostolic lord
of Kraków of Austria
of the Czechs (once again
of Kraków!)

so this isn't Denmark?
I'm in Poland
thank the Lord!

mini universe

the TV host in her
miniskirt crosses her legs
(pity it's not behind her neck)
tosses back her (dandruff-free) hair
pulls down her maxi mini
aligns her knees
her feet
un-decidedly
as befits
a well-mannered "feminist"
and starts to speak

"congratulations gentlemen
that's fabulous!
you yourselves
Polish astronomers
not just Engel and Boniek
and Copernicus
that's so cool!
so professor are you trying
to tell me . . . get outta here . . .
that this spherical system
has fifteen billion
stars sorry
spherical monads
let me ask which of you
gentlemen first got the idea"

The astronomer
with the beard opens his mouth
to say something about a black hole
but the "moderator" doesn't let him (speak)
it's such a neat idea
it gives me goosebumps
like Telimena in *Master Tadeusz*
professor you say it was an American
how do you explain the fact
that among astronomers there are so few
ladies
and so many Americans . . .

(laughter)
and are you professor
going to discover something new
in the superhole
maybe something metaphysical
tiny

that seems like nothing at all
and how did it all begin

well I have to disappoint you
the great explosion is just
an idea
whether it was an explosion or an act
of creation
we don't know

in that case professor let's come back down
to earth
among astronomers
is there a lot of rivalry
competition for titles awards
money
do astronomers have any
purely human foibles
why do women
so rarely look
through telescopes
is this a "male" profession
is there not something
we could call feminine astronomy
is antimatter
less interesting
to women
than conception
does a tiny something not
appear in the sky

ma'am!
present-day astronomers don't
see the sky! they're very busy
in modern astronomy
there's no time to gaze
at the stars
astronomy is not poetry
but teleology

what's needed is money
lots of money
for small amounts of money
you can see something
through a keyhole
in a word professor
it's all about money money
on the far side of the black hole
money's still what counts

you're terrifying me professor
professor I'm a woman
does an astronomer regard
sex
with an astronomical eye
or is he
just a regular macho man
who likes those things
I wish you all the stars in the sky
bye now

next week we'll be talking
about
genetics
and memetics
please join us for our
poetry club

it could be said that never
before have Polish astronomers

discovered so many planets
a veritable avalanche of planets comets
soon every Pole may have
his own planet
and the telescope will take its place
alongside the skis and the paintbox
ma'am
it's not so simple
a planet discovered last Tuesday
is five thousand
light years away
I find that hard to believe professor
surely you're joking!
yes yes
ma'am
competition in space
gossip in astronomy
and also relief and joy that we . . .

I'll keep my fingers crossed professor!

[January 2003]

the wheels are going round

yesterday between apocalypse and idyll
I heard across the ether
that the greenhouse effect
is caused
not only by the automobile industry
but also by cowpats
which release large amounts
of gas into the atmosphere
and so scientists are working on
a vaccine to prevent gas in cows
(while we are reminded in the process that
the number of cattle far exceeds
the needs of the human population)
I started thinking (the wheels are going round)
about the pats produced
by six billion people (more or less)
I came up with an idea for a virtual
worldwide global bank of gases
One could begin with the Bloating Foundation
"Prometheus-Gas" known for short as "Crapoco"
a gas pipeline
bypassing Russian Norway Iraq and the Tatra Mountain
National Park (as well as Southern Park in Wrocław
where they're putting up a statue of Chopin)
as a side product the anti-gas vaccine
could be marketed to retirees
and politicians

whose number far
exceeds the needs
of the country

Salvador Dalí
wrote years ago in a prophetic
rapture
"I had an aunt whom any kind
of scatology filled with disgust.
At the very idea that she might fart,
her eyes would fill with tears.
She was immensely proud that
she had never farted in her life . . ."

a vaccine against wind
will also take away
the raison d'être of various
Zoiluses who
are able to turn farts
into thunder (as they say in German
vom Furz ein Donner machen)

the wheels are going round

our gas
pipeline will bypass Kaliningrad
the statue of Kant Alaska Siberia
Belarus and Kraków
it will take into consideration
the strategic significance
of the Opole music festival

the wheels are going round, see?
I'm wasted here after all
it's high time

speech conversation dialogue

Humans have the gift of speech
This distinguishes people from animals

driver: "get the fuck
out of the car"
passenger: "you have no right"
driver: "in my cab
I got every right"

this dialogue concluded at the intersection
of Jana Pawła II
and Anielewicza Streets

cab drivers beat up a lady
professor from a western university
and boxed the ears
of a theater critic

the mayor of this Paris of the North
promised a thorough inquiry

three erotics

someone praised you sir
for a short and piquant erotic
I read it with interest

"Polyxena takes off her panties"

bring me heavier armor
I thought and wrote
two Gothic-Baroque erotics

"Petronella pulled on her panties"
"Greta Garbo steps out with no panties"

perhaps they'll make you smile

. . .

I was born a rhinoceros
with thick skin and a horn on my nose

I wanted to become a butterfly
but I was told
I have to be a rhinoceros

then I wanted to be
a songbird a stork
but I was told it wasn't possible

I asked why – the answer was
because you're a rhinoceros

I wanted to be a monkey
even a parrot!

but I was told . . . NO

I dreamt I had
soft pink skin
and a tiny nose like Cleopatra

but I was reminded that
I have really really thick skin
and that my horn is a mark of my identity

you were are and will be a rhinoceros
till the day you die

rhinoceros

my name is Tony
I'm a white rhino
I've never seen my homeland
of South Africa

my mother is called Tessa
I was born in a zoo
in a European capital

I was an only child
I never played with other little
rhinos

I was brought up behind heavy bars
with my mama I don't remember my daddy
mama told me that right after
their wedding night
daddy went back home to his city
supposedly his name was Diogenes

My name is Tony when
I was little I wanted to be
a butterfly but I was
told I was born a rhino
and have to be a rhino

I wanted to become a sparrow
because sparrows could fly

in and out of our cage they were free
they chirruped merrily so I wanted
to be a sparrow but I was
told I can't be
a sparrow

I asked why – because you're
a rhinoceros and you'll always be a rhinoceros
with thick skin and a horn on your nose
poor eyesight and a small brain

it seemed unfair to me

When I got bigger mama and I
started going out in the enclosure
nearby there lived a troop
of apes

apes are cheerful souls
they copulate blithely without
using condoms
they scratch their backsides delouse themselves eat their
parasites
masturbate without being afraid
they'll go to hell
though
the males are vicious arrogant
jealous
the females show their
colorful backsides not just
to the males but to the "whole world"

for which they do not receive large
fees from the television or
the playmate channel goodness how
talkative I'm being
we're visited
in the zoo by a strange
species of ape
these apes are wrapped in various
colored cloths
and they're bare
they have hair only on their heads
they carry their young in little carts

they're always drinking eating laughing
mama told me
that they're close relatives
of the orang-utans
they're called homosapiens
and a long time ago
they came down from the tree of knowledge
and went astray

In Southern Africa
these degraded apes organize
white rhino auctions
they sell our females
for fifty thousand pounds
they organize "safaris"
they use our horns to make
powder for their
impotent males

Mama told me that their females
are pregnant for nine months
Ours are pregnant for seventeen months
and during this time they don't smoke
don't drink vodka don't go to discos
don't watch horror films on TV

An old orang-utan told
me all kinds of terrible
things
about those apes and I thought
how good it is that I'm a rhino

last night I dreamt
I was a parrot
and I was terrified

embarrassment

Długa Street
"długa" meaning long
longer and longer
1 Długa Street
I've been invited
to the book fair
in Kraków

Długa Street
blades of grass between paving stones
moss on concrete
frail little flowers
in the gaps
between bricks

my guest room
is beneath a clock
in a tower
overlooking Basztowa Street
I get mixed up
count the steps
I'm thinking about Marta and Maria
Zosia Krystyna Małgorzata
Ewa and Renata
about Hania
I count the steps I count the years
148 steps

that's no joke
I breathe deeply
for the living and the dead
there's a kettle in my room
I'll make tea or coffee
invite the ladies from Art History
I have rolls cheese butter fruit
books flowers poems beer

our class never had
a "reunion"
it's high time
tempus fugit

the clock strikes twelve
I've been given an honorary doctorate
by the Jagiellonian University
why is no one coming
that's right Julian is a hundred
one's become a grandmother another's flown away
the charming dimples
in Marta's face have deepened

where did Professor Feliks Kopera come from
what's he doing here
he came from memory
but
how did he get up those winding stairs

I count the chimes of the clock
the book fair starts tomorrow
I'll sign copies of *little soul*
the scattered card index
gray zone

and *unease*

I sit at a plain booth
on a rickety chair
and start to feel embarrassed

above us there grow
supermarkets with baskets (!)
full of books
baskets with
bestsellers sanitary towels
for angels and fairies
a special on pretzels

J. K. Rowling
Paulo Coelho
Charlotte Link
and Stephen King
J. K. Rowling
J. K. Rowling

way
in the back the Dalai Lama
with his advice

from the heart
cannot keep up
with the lord of the rings
or with Queen Noor
or Ms. Nuala O'Faolain
with Hitler's manservant
or with Rowling Sabrina
Madonna
someone smiles at me

I hide my face

poetry graveyard

Hoesick's Poetry Library
Warsaw 1928

Kazimiera Alberti Revolt of the Avalanches My Film 2 złotys
Józef Birkenmajer By Street and Road 5 zł
Antoni Bogusławski Honor and Fatherland
Mieczysław Braun Trades Industries
Leon Choromański The Urn 6 zł
Wacław Denhoff-Czarnocki The Tramp 4 zł
Paul Géraldy You and I
Marja Grossek-Korycka A Lyrical Diary
Janina Hełm-Pirgo The Multicolored Sonata
Witold Hulewicz Instrumental Sonatas 4.50 zł
I. K. Iłłakowicz Weeping Bird The Golden Wreath
Maria Kasterska 1.50 zł
Wanda Miłaszewska God's Year 2 zł
Maria Pawlikowska Kisses The Fan Dance Card
Zofja Rościszewska Ribbons 6 zł

Antoni Słonimski From a Long Journey
Anatol Stern Race to the Pole
M. H. Szpyrkówna Poems 4 zł
Kazimierz Wroczyński Aeroplane
Emil Zegadłowicz The Juniper House
Stefan Napierski Letter to a Friend
"In Częstochowa (or Piotrków), remember, my dead cousin . . ."

recent poems

so what if it's a dream

I write on water

from a few phrases
a few poems
I build an ark

to save something
from the flood
that takes us by surprise
wipes us off the face
of the earth
when full of joy
we turn our faces
to the god of the sun
and to that God
who
"does not play dice"
we know Nothing
of cracks in the innards
of old mother earth
we raise towers
of sand
we build
on the verge
of life and death

our mother the earth
blue rounded

swathed in clouds
replete with the fertile waters
of life
full of volcanic fire
between two white ice-caps
green smelling of sap
flattened
after menstruations of war
after orgasms
of revolution
she falls asleep and dreams
of the Garden of Eden
of the gods on Olympus
of god in the highest
she breathes grows beautiful
gathers strength
flushes breathes deeply
rests after the creative work of evolution
like a mother wolf
she feeds human cubs
abandoned by the gods
neglecting
her responsibilities

My ark runs aground by degrees
on the sandbanks of words dreams

the gathered crowd
waits for a white dove
for fireworks and balloons

waits in curiosity
for human survivors
for animals and trees
moles and birds of paradise

But no one nothing
emerges from the ark

The drunken builder
sleeps amid naked bodies
that stink as they decompose

My name is Kanagawa
My name is Tsunami
laughs the young woman
she shows tattoos
on her backside and belly
prying cameras roam
over her pubic mound
filled with algae pearls
they glide across her labia
across her mouth
filled with shells with sand

The carrion stinks
providence watches web-eyed
over us
colorful bags with carcasses
of the drowned lie scattered in disarray
or stacked in containers

in refrigerators mass graves
pits cold-rooms
the waters have not yet fallen but
tourists are already on the beaches
beautiful young girls
sporting tee-shirts with logos

I have an urge for a Great Tsunami
perhaps you'd like to have a stormy
Tsunami with me

they sell gadgets
toys teddy bears
photos of decaying
corpses remains of animals humans
children are bought
children are sold
into houses of vice

Tsunami is a colorful media
spectacle on the surface
of infinity
Prying cameras rummage among the cadavers
lenses penetrating defenseless dead bodies
reporters and photographers
carry in their claws
fragments shreds pieces
of human flesh watches
heads arms rings hands
earrings innards notebooks cell phones

"everything" gradually
returns to normal
Tourists do not give up
the vacations they have paid for

it's good viewing it sets the adrenaline pumping
there are record ratings

I write on water
I write on sand
from a handful of salvaged words
from a few simple phrases
like the prose of carpenters
from a few naked poems
I build an ark
to save something
from the flood
that takes us by surprise
in broad daylight
or in the middle of the night
and wipes us from the face of the earth

I build my ark
a drunken boat
a little paper vessel
under red
black sails

So what if it's a dream

[Wrocław 2004–2005]

farewell to Raskolnikov

The waiter was pretending to wipe the table

I wanted to become a Napoleon
said Raskolnikov nonchalantly
but I only killed a louse

I had decided to act
with vigor to pave the way
for a great career

the air in the cheap cafe
was dense and rancid

on the table where I sat
with the "former" law student
was a glass of cloudy tea
on a small plate lay a squashed
stale napoleon
the greenish cream oozed from the pastry
like dried pus
sprinkled with icing sugar

I forgot about Raskolnikov
he forgot about me
everyone has their own affairs

a black fly that appeared
out of nowhere brought Raskolnikov to life
he moved aside the tea
and began waving the newspaper
containing his article

I knew he was aching
to show it me and even
read it aloud
the debut of a young
writer and scholar in the distant
hazy future

I remember that strange uncommon
feeling I shared it now
with Raskolnikov the excitement
my name in print!
youth has its entitlements

Forgive me it was amusing
naturally you wished to act
with vigor and so with an ax
not a fingernail (on the fingernail)
if Napoleon had wanted
to kill a louse he'd have used his fingernail
or one of his marshals

you're making fun of me he said
I know the whole thing was done
amateurishly and shoddily

to be honest I did it
out of boredom
I killed in my sleep
I killed a louse in my sleep
but the ax was real
I shot at lice
with a cannon
I was quite the Schiller
Raskolnikov lapsed into thought
then stood up and walked away
without shaking my hand
I remained alone with the napoleon
I paid for the tea
and left

Raskolnikov
was still standing in front of the cafe
which way are you headed I asked
"me? the other way" he said
nonchalantly and shrugged

he walked with lowered head
turned right into Sienna Street

a moment later
I heard shouts laughter
whistling ringing

I looked round

Raskolnikov was kneeling on the roadway
in a puddle of muddy snow
amid horse droppings
the new top hat Sonya bought him
set down on the cobblestones

he kissed the pavement three times made the sign of the cross
crossed himself . . . applause rang out
some guttersnipe knelt by him

I tried to raise him to his feet but he
fended me off gently and stood up
took my arm
and said confidentially
"here you have to avoid
being conspicuous . . .
Details, details
are the thing!
It's details that always
betray Everything . . ."
you to the right and me to the left
or the other way round . . . adieu
mon plaisir . . . till the next time we meet!

I never saw him again

[2004–2005]

depressions II

awakened I touch
my body
my face
the painful places of memory
I touch my skin

touch an alien body

I rub my eyes
but do not wish to open them
opening them
I rise but stay in bed the day rises
I look at my hand
say to myself: "dear lord!"
I hear that in the fields outside Cologne
a million young people
are searching for themselves God faith
the rag (yesterday's paper)
rustles underfoot I rise
start moving but not toward myself

depressions VII

"poor people"

Someone phones me
wants something I explain that
I'm here
that I'm not
that I
it's someone young
younger
he has plans
involving me
I explain that I have no
plans
in my thoughts I say
to myself be patient
polite
those young voices
scratch me
hurt me
those live voices
hurt me
why do young people
yell shout bellow
after all there's no
dudek or maradona here
małysz came in 20th or 26th
but he talks quietly
the poor kid

The Gates of Death

to the memory of Henryk Bereska

when I started writing poems
"everyone" was still alive
then they began to depart

the hardest task
is to pass through the gates of death
without the aid of an Angel

believers pass
through the gates of death
with eyes closed
once through
there is a smile on their lips

behind me I have a journey
growing longer
from hour to hour
before me I have
an ever shorter journey

faith in what exists
is knowledge not faith
but faith in what does not exist
is true faith

whoever believes God exists
needs no miracles
faith is the miracle

one who knows that love exists
has a duty to describe it
to let others see its image

The gates of death
The secret of their construction
is that the gates are not there
and at the same time they are
wide open to all
they are so narrow
that they must be squeezed through
in the sweat of one's brow
in bloody labor
for years on end squealing
or screaming in fear

fortunate those who die
in their sleep
their hand taken
by Eurydice
who is immortal
and weeps for she must
live on alone

Notes

the professor's knife
I: The Trains
Cyprian Kamil Norwid (1821–1883): the outstanding poet of the
    late Romantic period in Poland.
II: Columbus' Egg
"sugar fortifies": Polish advertising slogan from the 1950s.
    Melchior Wańkowicz (1892–1979) was a well-known author.
Father Robak and Jankiel: a Catholic priest and a Jewish
    innkeeper respectively, from the 1834 epic poem *Master
    Tadeusz* by Adam Mickiewicz (1798–1855): the major poet of
    the Romantic period. Konrad Wallenrod, a Teutonic knight,
    was the title character of a long poem by the same author
    from 1828.
III: Shades
Julian Przyboś (1901–1970): avant-garde poet. Bronisława
    (Bronia) was his wife.
Czarnolas: the country home of Jan Kochanowski (1530–1584),
    one of Poland's greatest poets, who wrote about sitting
    under the linden tree in his garden.
IV: The Discovery of the Knife
1968: in March 1968 there were student protests that led to an
    "anti-Zionist" clampdown by the government, forcing many
    Polish Jews to leave the country.
Zomo: the riot police.
VI: The Last Age
"*The iron age was last* [. . .]": from Ovid's *Metamorphoses* (author's
    note). The translation is adapted from that of A. S. Kline.
"the poet Jawień": pseudonym used by Karol Wojtyła (1920–
    2005), who later became Pope John Paul II.

gateway
"stone upon stone . . .": a children's song.

the mystery of the poem
"Ludwik Solski's Dressing Room": room in the Słowacki
    Theatre in Kraków, named after the famous Polish actor
    Ludwik Solski (1855–1954).
Extracts from Useful Books: anthology of world poetry compiled
    by Czesław Miłosz and published in 1994.

GRAY ZONE

gray zone
Antoni Kepiński (1918–1972): eminent psychiatrist and author.
Juliusz Słowacki (1809–1849): one of the leading poets and
    dramatists of the Romantic period.

I know nothing about you
White Marriage: 1975 play by Różewicz.

Oriole
Monika Żeromska (1913–2001): memoirist, daughter of Stefan
    Żeromski (1864–1925), the preeminent Polish writer of the
    early 20th century.
"a poem about a rose": a reference to "Dawn Day and Night
    with a Red Rose" from *the professor's knife* (author's note).
the Skamander poets: group of poets popular in the interwar
    period 1918–1939.

(Master Jakob Böhme)
Zgorzelec and Görlitz: adjacent towns on either side of the
    present Polish-German border.

conversation with Herr Scardanelli
Scardanelli was a pseudonym of the German poet Friedrich
    Hölderlin (1770–1843).

the spilling of blood
"caps with four corners": the four-cornered cap or *rogatywka* is
    the traditional headwear of Polish soldiers.

EXIT

my old Guardian Angel
"O heavenly angel guardian mine . . .": a bedtime prayer said by
    children.

golden thoughts against a black background
"golden thoughts" is a Polish expression meaning something
    like "quotable quotes."

à la Wyspiański
Stanisław Wyspiański (1869–1907): a Kraków painter and poet,
    one of the most significant figures in Polish culture.
Wawel: the former royal castle in Kraków.

(ever since the "little")
Albino Luciani: Pope John Paul I, who reigned for thirty-three
    days in 1978.

heart in mouth
Leopold Staff (1878–1957): outstanding poet of whom Tadeusz
    Różewicz is particularly fond.
Tadeusz Kotarbiński (1886–1981): a major Polish philosopher.
"three times yes": reference to a referendum in 1946 in which
    the Polish communists sought to legitimize their rule.
Roman Ingarden (1893–1970): influential Polish philosopher.

labyrinths
"leśmianek": or "little leśmian," a reference to Bolesław Leś-
mian (1878–1937), widely regarded as the most important
Polish poet of his time. His verse is characterized by
complex, innovative uses of language.

tempus fugit
"A cold coming . . ." from "Journey of the Magi" by T. S. Eliot.
"Fallen / angels / are like / [. . .] */ they fall drop by drop"*: this is the
entire text of the poem "Homework on the Topic of Angels"
from the poet's 1969 collection *Regio*.
"youth give me wings . . .": lines from "Ode to Youth" by Adam
Mickiewicz (1798–1855).
Jarosław Iwaszkiewicz (1894–1980): poet and writer, a leading
literary figure in the mid-century.

knowledge
This poem is a parody of "Paweł and Gaweł," a children's poem
by comic writer Aleksander Fredro (1793–1876). "Mr. Cogito"
frequently appears in the poetry of Zbigniew Herbert (1924–
1998).

I rub my eyes
"for bread good sir for bread": from a popular song about
emigration.
Telimena, Master Tadeusz, Robak: characters from Adam
Mickiewicz's *Master Tadeusz* (1834).
Emilia Plater (1806–1831): Polish national heroine who fought
and died in the 1831 November Uprising.
"painted uhlans": referring to Polish soldiers (from a popular
song)
"our good emperor": the emperor of Austria-Hungary.

you can't scare me
King Władysław the Short (1260–1333): King of Poland from
    1320.

RECENT POEMS

depressions VII
Jerzy Dudek: a well-known Polish soccer player.
Adam Małysz: a champion ski-jumper.

The Gates of Death
Henryk Bereska (1926–2005): an eminent translator of Polish
    literature into German.

DATE DUE
